Framing
Marginality

Interpretations

This series provides clearly written and up-to-date introductions to recent theories and critical practices in the humanities and social sciences.

General Editor
Ken Ruthven (University of Melbourne)

Advisory Board
Tony Bennett (Griffith University)
Penny Boumelha (University of Adelaide)
John Frow (University of Queensland)
Sneja Gunew (University of Victoria, British Columbia)
Kevin Hart (Monash University)
Robert Hodge (University of Western Sydney)
Terry Threadgold (Monash University)

Already published:
Cultural Materialism, by Andrew Milner
Metafictions?, by Wenche Ommundsen
A Foucault Primer, by Alec McHoul and Wendy Grace
Nuclear Criticism, by Ken Ruthven
After Mabo, by Tim Rowse
Framing and Interpretation, by Gale MacLachlan and Ian Reid
Masculinities and Identities, by David Buchbinder
The Architecture of Babel, by Damien Broderick

In preparation:
Postmodern socialism, by Peter Beilharz
Theories of desire, by Patrick Fuery
Post-colonial literature, by Anne Brewster

Framing
Marginality

Multicultural literary studies

Sneja Gunew

MELBOURNE UNIVERSITY PRESS
1994

First published 1994
Designed by Mark Davis/text-art
Typeset in 10½ point Garamond by Mark Davis/text-art
Printed in Malaysia by SRM Production Services Sdn Bhd for
Melbourne University Press, Carlton, Victoria 3053

Distribution agents
Australia: Penguin Books Australia Ltd,
487 Maroondah Highway, PO Box 257,
Ringwood, Victoria 3134

ISSN 1039-6128

National Library of Australia Cataloguing-in-Publication Entry

Gunew, Sneja.
    Framing marginality: multicultural literary studies.
    Bibliography.
    Includes index.
    ISBN 0 522 84639 4.
    1. Australian literature—Minority authors—History and
criticism. 2. Minorities in literature. I. Title. (Series:
Interpretations).
A820.9920693

Contents

Acknowledgements .... *vii*

Preface.. *xi*

1 Introduction: From Migrant Writing to Ethnic
  Minority Literatures *1*
  A brief history of Australian multicultural
  literary studies... *1*
  Anthologies *6*
  A Bibliography of Australian Multicultural Writers
  and the multicultural literature collection at Deakin
  University *10*
  Theoretical structures *11*
  Publishing/editing/reviewing................................. *15*
  Policy work *15*
  Reinventing the national culture *18*
  Redefining the public sphere *22*

Part I Framing Marginality

2 Marginal Positions: Constructing Cultural
  Differences on Various 'Posts' *27*
  Framing aesthetics *27*
  Universal culture.. *28*
  Civilised (male) subjects *29*

Contents

Alterity 32
National cultures: Englishness/English studies 36
Post-colonial critiques 38
Minority cultures/literatures 41
Situated knowledge: the local 44
Multiculturalism: between ethnicity and race 46

3 The Question of Authenticity: Feminist Theory
and Minority Writing 53

Part II Reading for Cultural Difference

4 In Journeys Begin Dreams: Antigone Kefala
and Ania Walwicz 71

5 The Grotesque Migrant Body: Rosa Cappiello's
Oh Lucky Country 93

6 Homeland, Nostalgia, the Uncanny: The Work
of Anna Couani 111

Notes 132
Bibliography 136
Index 153

Acknowledgements

The daughter of 'Displaced Persons' is not able to take anything for granted, least of all that of being naturalised, even if the documents are there to prove it. Embarking yet again on both emigration and immigration there is one certainty, that one neither leaves nor arrives. Undoubtedly Australia will always be the place that has implicated me in particular formations, embedded shards of identity in certain ways. Some of those fragments are offered here and shaped into a kind of coherence. The work on which this book is based has taken place over fourteen years. It breaks new ground in so far as it has drawn attention to a neglected area of Australian writing. Since the shape of this book existed a decade ago, before there were debates conducive to its publication, the next-best alternative was to publish various sections over the years in order to help generate an appropriate critical climate. The material here is reshaped by current discussions and contemporary theoretical emphases and frameworks. Questions of marginalities, cultural difference, minority writings, ethnicity and race comprise the urgent debates of the final decade of the millennium.

It is in the nature of such new enterprises to involve many people and much networking. My gratitude extends to many: to my colleagues at Deakin over fourteen years, especially to Ian Reid, Brian Edwards, Wenche Ommundsen, Hazel Rowley in Literature, and in the former School of Humanities to Louise

Johnson, Li Veit-Brause, Gerry Kunstler, Ron Gilbert, Philipa Rothfield, Purusottama Bilimoria and, in the wider Deakin, Fazal Rizvi, Pam Maclean, Gill Gartlan. For their help and enthusiasm in establishing the Multicultural Literature Collection my thanks to Margaret Cameron, Helen Livingston and Cate Richmond and to Hass Dellal and the Australian Bicentennial Multicultural Foundation for making this dream possible. My gratitude to Peter Lane and the crew in Media for their patience with my attempts to move into video. Much conceptual territory was clarified in the process.

My respect for and thanks to colleagues in the wider networks who are doggedly trying to keep the debates going: Con Castan, Kateryna Longley, Ivor Indyk, Jim Kable, Chitra Fernando, Helen Nickas, Gaetano Rando, Walter Veit, Yasmine Gooneratne, Manfred Jurgensen, Adolfo Gentile, Mimis Sophocleus, Andrew Jakubowitz, Mary Kalantzis.

To the new generation my best wishes: Efi Hatzimanolis, Nikos Papastergiadis, Dina Dounis, Suvendrini Perera, Joseph Pugliese, Shirley Tucker, Mirjana Lozanovska.

My particular gratitude to those friends who convinced me to persevere and kept the issues alive through their own passionate engagement and commitment: Antigone Kefala, Jan Mahyuddin, Anna Couani, Peter and Tes Lyssiotis, Loló Houbein, Paul Carter, Liz Gertsakis, Jolanta and Jurgis Janavicius, Alexandra Büchler.

Colleagues who gave their encouragement and support from other institutional embeddings: Susan Sheridan, Liz Grosz, Anna Gibbs, Anna Yeatman, Ken Ruthven, David Carter, John Frow, Meaghan Morris, Homi Bhabha, Michele Grossman, and Mary Dimech of the Australia Council. Particular thanks to Carole Ferrier and Bronwyn Levy who aired many early attempts in *Hecate*. Thanks to Judith Brett for early encouragement to publish in *Meanjin* and to Jenny Lee for facilitating later cogitations in that journal.

My eternal gratitude to the stalwart efforts of those who typed my many papers and chapters over the years: Judy Barber, Judy Waldie, Val Lestrange. And particular thanks to Alex Thomas and Marian Boreland for their cheerful and willing help above and beyond the usual duties of research assistants.

My special gratitude for their support in all the other intangible and essential ways to my family and to Terence Greer.

Acknowledgement is also due to the following individuals and companies for permission to reproduce copyright material: Antigone Kefala for 'Concert'; Ania Walwicz for material from *Writing* and for poems published in *Displacements 2* and *Mattoid 13*; Angus & Robertson for material from Ania Walwicz's *Boat*; Columbia University Press for J. Kristeva's *Powers of Horror*; Cornell University Press for A. Jardine's *Gynesis*; Hale & Iremonger for Antigone Kefala's *Absence* and *European Notebook*; J. M. Dent for Dante's *Inferno*; Masterthief Enterprises and Sea Cruise Books for Anna Couani and Peter Lyssiotis's *The Harbour Breathes*; Oxford University Press for K. Silverman's *The Subject of Semiotics*; Rigmarole Books for Anna Couani's *Italy* and *Were All Women Sex-mad?*; University of Queensland Press for Rosa Cappiello's *Oh Lucky Country*.

Other versions of some of the chapters have appeared in the following: Chapter 3 in S. Sheridan (ed.), *Grafts: Feminist Cultural Criticism*, London: Verso, 1989; Chapter 4 in B. Marshall and D. Brooks (eds), *Poetry and Gender*, Sydney: Hale & Iremonger, 1988; Chapter 5 in *Meanjin*, 44, 1, 1985; Chapter 6 in P. Foss (ed.) *Island in the Stream*, Sydney: Pluto Press, 1988.

Particular thanks to the following in helping with revisions of this Chapter 6: Paul Foss, Anna Couani, John Hutnyk, Geraldine Kunstler and Nikos Papastergiadis.

Preface

'Multicultural' literature is defined differently according to its national contexts. In the United States, for example, it appears to be distinguished from 'ethnic' literature, the former signalling the writings of those who are termed visible minorities and the latter indicating those who to some extent choose to affiliate with their ethnic roots but are not placed in the position of being the easy focus of racist projections. Thus there is a distinction between 'ethnicity' and 'race' as determining cultural factors. In Australia the term is reserved for those who write from outside the prevailing Anglo-Celtic traditions, that is, writers who have a privileged relation to languages and cultures other than those deriving from England and Ireland, the point of embarkation for most of Australia's first colonisers. Intimacy with other languages and traditions comes either from being born overseas or from having parents or grandparents who migrated from places other than England or Ireland. Clearly the degree to which these other languages or literary traditions inform writing produced in an Australian context varies considerably, and research and analysis in this area have barely begun.

The term 'migrant writing' is used not simply to designate those writers born overseas, but rather misleadingly to describe the writings of all those Australians perceived as not belonging to the literary and cultural traditions deriving from England and Ireland. Thus even a third-generation writer like Anna Couani continues to be labelled a migrant writer because her name signals her descent from Greek and Polish forebears. Related expressions such as 'ethnic' or 'multicultural' writer are coded terms for continuing to maintain these divisions. For the purposes of developing more precise analytical concepts pertaining to Australia's national literature it would be more useful to distinguish between writers who are overseas-born, and thus might be expected to be overtly concerned with the experience of migration and its attendent cultural dislocations, and those writers who have intimate access to languages and cultures that do not derive from England or Ireland and who may or may not write in English.

If the designations 'ethnic' or 'multicultural' are to have any real intellectual purchase they would need to include the specific cultural traditions of those whose ethnicity currently remains invisible, that is, the English (including the Welsh, Scots, etc.) and the Irish. One could argue that Irish ethnicity might be described as being highly visible to the extent that it has to some degree become synonymous with what is usually defined as quintessentially Australian culture, particularly in its folk-life manifestations (e.g. folk-music, ballads).

Certain conventions appear to be attached to migrant writing. Under this rubric, writers, particularly those who draw attention to their awareness of languages other than English, are perceived in the main as dealing simply with their own life-stories, as providing material primarily of interest to sociologists or oral historians. The playfulness or reflexivity in their writings, manifest for example in the work of Rosa Cappiello and Ania Walwicz, remains largely unacknowledged. Those few writers who are generally recognised to constitute the field of 'migrant writing' are usually restricted to a realist mode established by the first writer to be thus considered, Judah Waten, whose *Alien Son* was seen as the paradigmatic text.

Current bibliographical work which focuses on writers from backgrounds other than English reveals that they number around nine hundred such writers, which is not surprising considering that there are at present over sixty language groups in Australia. If one takes into account the second and third generation, roughly one-third of Australians derive from other than English-speaking cultural traditions. Clearly, a separate group with distinctive cultural characteristics is constituted by the Aboriginal or indigenous Australians.

The term favoured throughout this study as a way of negotiating the local and global contradictions set up by established terms such as 'migrant', 'ethnic' or 'multicultural' writers is 'ethnic minority writers' (Padolsky, 1991).

Helpful references for Australian multicultural literary studies:
S. Gunew, L. Houbein, A. Karakostas-Seda and J. Mahyuddin (eds) (1992) *A Bibliography of Australian Multicultural Writers*, Deakin University: Centre for Studies in Literary Education.
S. Gunew and K. O. Longley (eds) (1992) *Striking Chords: Multicultural Literary Interpretations*, Sydney: Allen & Unwin.
The latter includes further bibliographic information covering the field.

1

Introduction: From Migrant Writing to Ethnic Minority Literatures

A brief history of Australian multicultural literary studies

Whatever else we may feel about postmodernist and post-colonialist debates, they have undoubtedly precipitated a widespread acceptance of the fact that positionality—where you stand in relation to what you say—is central to the construction of knowledge. In other words, they have made it more difficult to talk about literature in terms of universal propositions, or about texts without reference to their contexts. This has resulted in an impetus to consider local elements: histories, socio-politics, and ethnic specificities. At the same time, and fortuitously, this development has also been anti-nationalist in some respects by not being limited to the local in any parochial sense. Instead we have become aware of different levels of constructing such unities, and of the investments of power these bring into play. In spite of rhetoric to the contrary, no nation or language has ever been a naturally unified entity (Anderson, 1991), although some have attempted to imply this by means of an emblematic iconography based on imagined or actual earthly boundaries (Boelhower, 1987). This applies even to the island kingdom of Britain, to Englishness and the English language. English can be said to have sprung many leaks, and indeed to have been always the product of spillage from many languages and cultures; consequently we now tend to differentiate, for example, between English literature and literatures in English. Considerations of perspective and positionality, and the relative status of knowledge production, have engendered an awareness of diasporic webs and connections created by means of those many sign-systems we call languages.

To talk about 'multiculturalism' is to be faced with all these elements. Although the term resonates globally, it has very specific local inflections. In the United Kingdom it refers to Black–White relations, where 'Black' encompasses Africans, Caribbeans and Asians. It tends to refer to the old Commonwealth, or, at the very least, to those peoples who have been recently oppressed by colonialism (Anthias and Yuval-Davis, 1992). In the US it refers to historically marginalised groups: Blacks (African-Americans), Hispanics and to some extent Asians (from Pakistan and the Indian subcontinent as well as from Vietnam, Korea, etc.) and Arabs. In Canada multiculturalism, in spite of its history,[1] denotes those who are not included in the English–French axis. In New Zealand the term barely circulates, because it is perceived as detracting from an emphasis on biculturalism which is structured around Maori claims for sovereignty. In response to this last instance we realise that multiculturalism needs to be differentiated from the struggles by various indigenous peoples for independence.

In Australia the Aborigines emphatically distance themselves from multiculturalism, which they perceive as being predicated on various cultures of migration. Having marked this distinction, we should note also that multiculturalism in Australia incorporates all those *other* than the original settler-colonising groups composed mainly of people from the UK and Ireland. Because the shorthand (and contested) term for this group is 'Anglo-Celtic', 'multicultural' tends to translate into 'non-Anglo-Celts'. In New Zealand the comparable term, Pakeha, also functions primarily in relation to groups descended from the British, and thus occludes other kinds of cultural difference. Multiculturalism in Australia has tended to refer to Europeans, and initially to those Northern groups which are often excluded from multiculturalism in the North American or the British sense because they are associated with privilege and the colonising process. They comprise those who, after World War II, became refugees and 'displaced persons' (DPs). Broadly speaking, after that early postwar period the subsequent immigrants consisted first of those classified as economic migrants (mainly from Southern Europe), and later of people fleeing from various wars in Hungary, Vietnam, Lebanon and soon, no doubt, the former Yugoslavia. Increasingly it has come to include a wide range of over a hundred ethnic groups (Jupp, 1988). Because Australia is unrelentingly an English-speaking country, ethnic diversity has had a number of ramifications, and ethnic groups have functioned to some degree as a way of measuring symptoms associated with national aspirations and anxieties.

Why should we study these 'ethnic minority writings', and is this phrase the best way of referring to them? The Canadian critic Francesco Loriggio (1990a) has made the point that such writings serve to connect literature and aesthetics to history, for by summoning up the history of minorities they draw attention to that which mainstream history has excluded. In Australia these writings have had currency first as 'migrant writing', then as 'ethnic writing', and more recently as 'multicultural writing'. Each of these terms has signalled the alterity of various writings produced in Australia but perceived as 'other' *(alter)* than the Anglo-Celtic norm. The problems centre upon the paradox of emphasising the difference of that which, eventually, you are seeking to incorporate within the mainstream. Once again, Francesco Loriggio aptly summarises the range of work which faces those involved in mapping ethnic minority writings:

> One of the most interesting aspects of ethnic literature as a field of study is the obligations it entails. The critic is forced to work on many levels simultaneously. S/he must name the texts, disseminate them, and, at the same time, at this particular stage of the game, define them, situate them within the literary agenda of the century and the debate it has fostered. Editing, translating, the journalistic piece or the one-page review are not beyond his/her ken. And neither are the more ethereal spheres of his/her discipline. In short, s/he must document the

existence of the corpus, of the tradition, while grappling with the criteria that establish them. (Loriggio, 1990a:21)

In other words it has been necessary both to assemble the work and to find the conceptual tools to analyse it. The biggest difference between the Canadian and Australian experience, for example, is in sheer critical mass; more people are working on these issues in Canada, and the Canadians have achieved much more detailed work on the histories and writings of specific cultural groups (Gunew, 1993a). Comparable work in Australia has been much more sporadic and *ad hoc*, and bedevilled by a slightly different battery of obstacles and prejudices (Gunew, 1992; 1993b). For a start, Canada is not as unrelentingly English as Australia. Such divisions as are acknowledged in Australia focus on splits between the Anglo-Protestants (usually middle-class) and the Irish Catholic working class, and more recently on a belated attempt to reconcile rifts between the settler-colonisers and the indigenous peoples. Within those divisions, other groups have been lost, or seen as too 'other' and foreign. The very fact that Canada has two founding languages and cultures has made quite a difference to the level of tolerance for non-English cultures and languages.

Another difference is in a sense symptomatic of these conditions, namely that a great deal is revealed, as always, through nomenclature. The general shorthand term for minority ethnic writings in Australia is still 'migrant literature'. In other words it is seen as transitory and not really rooted in the place at all. It is often talked about in the marketplace as a literature that deals with themes, characters and events situated 'outside' Australia.[2] It is to rectify these absurdities that a relatively small group of academics has been labouring to change this picture and align it more closely with comparable international models (Gunew and Longley, 1992b). Roughly five kinds of activity have been involved in setting up multicultural literary studies in Australia: the production of anthologies and bibliographies; the establishment of collections of multicultural literature; the framing of theoretical structures for the study of such materials, including the setting up of academic courses on it; reviewing and publishing multicultural writing; and working with government agencies on multicultural policy. The first three could be termed the general strategy of making an absence visible. It is something learnt from the institutional establishment of women's writing a few decades ago.[3]

Thinking about cultural difference in an Australian context began around 1979, when questions of 'positionality' or 'perspectivism' were just beginning to stimulate a major debate in cultural studies. In this regard, Francesco Loriggio (1990b:89) pertinently suggests that 'point of view, positioning of oneself or the subject matter are at once the ultimate dimension and the ultimate device of ethnicity'.

During the 1970s multiculturalism was being consolidated as government policy. Inevitably, the dominant emphases were mobilised around issues of social justice, such as access and equity, and a welfare model of 'lack' or 'disadvantage'. In other words, Australians were asked to think in terms of a migrant/ethnic 'problem' which led inevitably to the construction of migrants or ethnics as *themselves* the problem. It was never a question of what these people could contribute to the nation through their different cultures and languages. Instead it became a question of what had to be sliced off the national funding cake in order to keep them quiet, and to lend credibility to the image of Australia as a democratic and equitable nation. It is crucial to distinguish here between those government policies and institutions which are designed to manage cultural diversity and the claims for cultural involvement which emanate from the various ethnic groups themselves. The politics of these two areas are quite different, and often in conflict; but opponents of multiculturalism invariably merge them, and indict both for dividing the nation.

Multiculturalism intersects, but is not synonymous with, immigration. As has often been pointed out, if immigration were to stop tomorrow there would still be multiculturalism. In order to understand the contexts within which multicultural literature operates it is useful to familiarise oneself with the history of the immigration of culturally diverse groups in Australia. The *National Agenda for a Multicultural Australia*, which the Office of Multicultural Affairs published in 1989, provides a state definition of multiculturalism, and there is in addition the officially endorsed encyclopedia edited by Jupp (1988). But of course it is not only the state or official policy-makers who define these social realities. Fazal Rizvi, for example, traces the movement from assimilation to multiculturalism in the following manner:

> The policy of assimilation was clearly and unambiguously designed to preserve the hegemony of the Anglo-Australian ruling class. Yet it was 'sold' to the immigrants in a language that suggested meritocracy, egalitarianism and equality of opportunity. According to the rhetoric used, immigrant groups were encouraged to assimilate into a homogeneous culture so that they, too, could have an opportunity to take an equal and informed part in the maintenance of Australian society. (Rizvi, 1989:8)

Multiculturalism as a policy emerged in the 1960s. According to Andrew Jakubowitz's critique, 'multiculturalism functions as an ideology by appearing to act on behalf of the disadvantaged migrants, though in reality it leaves essential social relations and an unequal distribution of power in Australia unaltered' (ibid.:16).

Anthologies

Once migrants and their descendants became interested in the whole field of 'migrant writing', it was clear that the necessary first stage in the enterprise was what has been termed the strategy of visibility. At that time, around 1979, it was a case of having to sift through old journals and anthologies in order simply to come up with the names of writers and examples of their work. In my own case it resulted in the editing and co-editing of four anthologies of multicultural writing (Gunew, 1981, 1987a; Gunew and Mahyuddin, 1988; Couani and Gunew, 1988). Curriculum work on what were then known simply as 'migrant writers' was grounded more easily in interdisciplinary cultural studies than traditional literary studies, because, inescapably, this writing could make sense only within the context of the history and politics of postwar migration. In my own case, the actual context was the first-year course on narratology in Deakin University's undergraduate literature major. Students in this interdisciplinary course were exposed to various forms of narrative, including film and visual material. Within the framework of an Australian oral history project, they were asked to research the Depression era, using family and friends for interviews. Realising that people like myself would not find such an enterprise easy, it struck me that a comparable and more appropriate task for students from non-Anglo-Celtic families to undertake might be research into Australian postwar migration. From this simple idea, course material was produced. It comprised two videos and an anthology called *Displacements: Migrant Writers* (Gunew, 1981), which incorporates a wide variety of narratives dealing with the experience of migration, ranging from relatively unmediated first-person accounts to complex texts which use unreliable narrators and multiple levels of irony.

The videos were to some extent self-reflexive examinations of the so-called authenticity of two formats, the interview and the documentary. Since then, many films, ranging from the realist to the experimental, have dealt with multicultural hybridity (Blonski, 1993). The second anthology was entitled *Displacements 2: Multicultural Storytellers* (Gunew, 1987a), and the changed subtitle illustrates a necessary historical shift in approach. It became clear to me that this project of 'visibility' needed to distinguish between migrants writing in the main about the experience of migration, and works by non-Anglo-Celtic writers (often second- and third-generation) which are distinguished by their intimate links to linguistic and literary traditions other than those deriving from England or Ireland. The term 'migrant', as pointed out above, conjures up subjects whose presence in the dominant culture is merely temporary, and whose orientation is towards a past nostalgically conceived of as a lost motherland and mother tongue. This precariousness is further signalled by such widely used bureaucratic terms as NESB (non-English-speaking background), an exclusionary acronym which indicates an insecure hold on the only language which is the measure of linguistic competence in Australia, namely English.

'Anglo-Celtic' is also a fraught term, given the ways in which the battles between England and Ireland have been fought out symbolically in the Australian arena. We need also to acknowledge the fact that Britain itself is divided culturally as a nation, and that Welsh and Scottish claims need to be separated out (Nairn, 1977). This study uses the designation 'Anglo-Celtic' to indicate not only a British-derived culture based on the use of the English language but also certain political and cultural institutions, and especially a tradition of education in 'English studies'. Those who simply use the term 'Anglo' or 'Anglocentric' (Castles et al., 1988) leave out the crucial Celtic component in Australian culture. Indeed, in Australia, dissidence has been synonymous to some degree with Irish working-class and Catholic groups; while I have no wish to play down the differences between 'Anglo' and 'Irish Catholic' groups, I want to focus here on other forms of dissidence and difference. No other shorthand term than 'Anglo-Celtic' indicates so aptly a prevailing cultural nostalgia that gestures towards an old country which is always either England or Ireland, and which characterises the dominant ethnic groups here. Indeed, the Celtic portion of the term indicates an efficient hijacking of Australian culture by the Irish, who have managed to convince many of us that much of what we think of as quintessentially Australian culture—the laconic humour, the folk-music and many canonical Australian writers—derives directly from Ireland. This study retains the term 'Anglo-Celtic' (with these cautions) to differentiate between the cultural contributions of those whose linguistic and cultural traditions derive from England or Ireland, and those who are linked to the sixty or more other language groups which have colonised Australia. Non-Anglo-Celts need to be as vigilant as second-wave feminists were to the politics of language and naming.

By the time the second anthology was produced in the late 1980s, there was a much greater mix of first- and second-generation non-Anglo-Celtic writers. Concerns were no longer limited to the experience of migration. This was the era of popular stage shows such as *Wogs Out of Work*, which resulted in the television comedy series *Acropolis Now*. In popular culture an aggressive counter-discourse was beginning to emanate from inner-city Melbourne and Sydney youths of non-Anglo-Celtic background. It became easier to foreground questions of mediation, in the sense that prevailing stereotypes of the national culture were already being interrogated by second-generation writers perched strategically and knowingly between cultures. Their intervention also cast doubts on the adequacy of categories such as class and gender, which had become an acknowledged part of the critical vocabulary. Ethnicity or cultural difference immediately inflects both class and gender in quite particular ways.

In the literary domain, second-generation Mediterraneans or Southern Europeans are now relatively famous: I have in mind the performance pieces of Π. O. (Pi. O.) and Komninos, and the writings of Angelo Loukakis and George Papaellinas as well as of Anna-Maria Dell'oso and Zeny Giles. Unlike their parents' generation, which was made up of rural and urban working- or lower middle-class people in a world of milkbars and fish'n'chip shops, they themselves have been upwardly mobile aspirants to full metropolitan and bourgeois status.

The appearance in the mid-1980s of Manfred Jurgensen's *Outrider* (a journal dedicated initially to publishing multicultural writing) indicated a different perception of multicultural literature by linking it with bourgeois culture by way of *Weltliteratur.* Within the ambit of the 'best' of 'world literature', the journal now publishes overseas writers and Anglo-Celtic as well as non-Anglo-Celtic Australian writers. This represents another tactic for integrating multicultural concerns into Australian literature, but it does not fundamentally alter the premises upon which Australia's national culture is founded. In other words, it merely adds some more writers without considering the fact that this 'supplement' redefines the whole domain of Australian literature. It also has a quite markedly Eurocentric framework.

In the midst of these concerns, the third anthology, *Beyond the Echo: Multicultural Women's Writing* (Gunew and Mahyuddin, 1988), proclaimed itself as emphatically *not* an anthology of migrant writing. It signalled a desire, that is, to be considered as part of literature rather than sociology. The primary function of both this volume and the fourth anthology, *Telling Ways: Australian Women's Experimental Writing* (Couani and Gunew, 1988), is to insert the writings of non-Anglo-Celtic women into the mushrooming domain of women's writing. By this stage Australian feminist debates were increasingly concerned with the differences between women: they constituted another version of the dismantling of a universalist cultural politics. Although the publisher of *Beyond the Echo* wanted an anthology organised thematically around the migrant experience, we did not provide one. Our anthology questions various generic expectations of women's writing: that it will be confessional or autobiographical; that it is automatically authentic and unmediated by conventions; that 'NESB' means linguistic deficiency and so on. In *Telling Ways* the particular focus of experimental writing makes this point even more strongly. I should add that many writers first published in *Beyond the Echo* went on to produce books of their own, thus vindicating the production of anthologies as a visibility strategy.

A Bibliography of Australian Multicultural Writers and the multicultural literature collection at Deakin University

In 1992 there appeared the first comprehensive bibliography of multicultural writers in Australia (Gunew, Houbein, Karakostas-Seda and Mahyuddin, 1992a), which contains around nine hundred authors and numbers three hundred pages of double-column entries. Substantially accumulated by Jan Mahyuddin and co-ordinated by myself, it is based on earlier work by Loló Houbein and Alexandra Karakostas-Seda, but differs in deliberately including second- and even third-generation writers. The project is immersed in the politics of taxonomies and categorisation. The presence of second- and third-generation writers emphasises the continuing necessity to move beyond the category of the 'migrant' so that questions of cultural difference infiltrate all future considerations of the national literature. The bibliography includes some listing of the critical reception of these writers, together with information concerning translators. We found that about 33 per cent published in English, 32 per cent in English and other languages, and 35 per cent in languages other than English. We also included quite well-known Australian writers such as David Malouf and Elizabeth Jolley as well as Henry Lawson, doyen of an earlier era, in order to point out the need to reassess all Australia's literature in terms of the whole range of cultural influences which have gone into its production. The object was both to facilitate analyses of ethnic writers in Australia and to raise the question of ethnicity in all Australian literature. The information collected as part of this project is in the process of being mainstreamed into the BALP (Bibliography of Australian Literature Project) database (National Centre for Australian Studies, Monash University). While it was being compiled, this bibliography—funded by the Australian Bicentennial Multicultural Foundation—formed the basis for the first comprehensive collection of multicultural literature in this country. Judging from enquiries received from Germany, England, Japan, the US and Canada, there is clearly a growing body of critics interested in diasporic cultures, such as those for example, of Italian or Greek writers in Australia. At present the Australian National Library's catalogues of their holdings in foreign languages do not specify whether writers are Australian, so it is extremely difficult to carry out research in the field of Australian writing in languages other than English. In addition, work on the bibliography made us acutely aware that irreplaceable papers and manuscripts were being lost because there was no adequately co-ordinated institutional interest in them. Deakin University's multicultural literature collection is on the national system and can be accessed nationally and internationally. It is also generating a catalogue and database which will be invaluable to future researchers. The multicultural literature collection, in conjunction with the bibliography, forms the base for future research into the different linguistic and cultural groups in Australia, and particularly those originating in the nineteenth century. Eventually it will enable much more precise statements to be made about the impact of cultural difference on Australian culture.

Theoretical structures

Critics of ethnic minority writings commonly assume that poststructuralist theories are inappropriate for examining what are deemed for the most part to be unproblematic first-person narratives or community histories. According to the Canadian critic Joseph Pivato, for example, 'the work of the ethnic writers has an immediate grassroots nature that demands that these texts be read on their own terms before they can be related to existing models' (Pivato, 1994). While it is true that we should exercise caution before imposing critical structures on such writing, I find Pivato's phrase 'on their own terms' problematic, since it is precisely such assumptions (reduced to the narrowest terms) which have impeded the reception of multicultural literature in Australia. In an early attempt to tackle the theoretical issues here I argued, on the basis of Jacques Derrida's concept of the 'supplement', that the addition of so-called migrant writing would eventually redefine the premises governing the formation of Australian literature (Gunew, 1985). Later research has simply confirmed this notion, and emphasised the continuing need to wrest these writings away from their allegedly 'natural' place in oral history and sociology, where they are read simply for their historical or sociological content, and in ways that render their textuality invisible. In other words, the old battles to claim these writings as part of literature are still being fought. It is also necessary to reiterate the need to differentiate between migrant writing and non-Anglo-Celtic writing. Recent forays have entered into debates around the formation of national literatures (Gunew, 1990a).

What critical apparatus exists for speaking about minority literatures, or 'literatures of lesser diffusion' or 'other solitudes' as they are referred to in Canada? 'Ethnic minority literatures' (Padolsky, 1991, 1992) is a useful phrase because it implies that there is always an ethnic majority literature, and thus draws attention to the question of ethnicity in *all* literature. In other words, it acts as a reminder of what we have learnt from various recent emancipatory struggles, namely the primary need to deconstruct the hegemonic centre.

The word 'minority' also alludes to an influential study by Deleuze and Guattari (1986), who use the example of Franz Kafka to distinguish between a minor literature (in a major language) and a literature of minorities (written in a minor language). They also introduce the useful (and highly complex) concept of the 'deterritorialisation' of the dominant language by minority languages. Unmoored from within, the dominant language loses its power as a kind of Adamic naming and hence possession of the world.

Post-colonial criticism (deriving from the work of Frantz Fanon, Edward Said, Gayatri Spivak, Homi Bhabha and others) has also

12

been influential in linking questions of language and representation with claims to cultural sovereignty or enfranchisement. It was used initially of colonised indigenous peoples; but more recently, and rather disturbingly, it is being applied in an almost depoliticised sense to those descendants of the colonisers who are now trying to cut free of various imperial mother countries. This is certainly occurring in Australia, where post-colonialism has been appropriated to some degree by these interest groups, who position themselves on the one hand in relation to mother England and on the other hand (and to some degree sentimentally) in relation to Aboriginal Australia. Such moves eclipse both postwar immigration history and a range of positions relating to cultural difference. To some extent, 'cultural difference' as an analytic category emerges out of post-colonialism, but it comes also out of feminist debates about sexual difference, as well as, in turn, analyses of racial difference in the Black movement. These theories and theorists are discussed in greater detail in the next two chapters.

From the very beginning, post-structuralist theories have proved useful in defining this new terrain, because they undo the very notion that pure and separate categories exist within aesthetics or, indeed, cultural politics. Aspects of deconstruction, psychoanalysis, feminism and post-colonialism thus helped demonstrate that these writings are available to high literary theory. It was equally clear that they are amenable to those current theories of the postmodern which focus on such matters as the 'decentred' subject, anti-narrative fragmentation, and a scepticism about master-narratives (Lyotard, 1984). Post-structural psychoanalysis has also proved important because it provides the most sophisticated framework for theorising the formation of subjectivity in relation to unconscious processes, such as the idea of entering the symbolic order of language. Jacques Lacan's famous dictum that 'the unconscious is structured like a language' raised the possibility that the unconscious may well be formed in relation to particular languages rather than to language-in-general. This in turn provokes many questions about the silences in classic Lacanian theory, which remains remarkably resistant to historically specific enquiries.

With hindsight, the degree of institutional resistance these projects attracted was hardly surprising, because the work was occurring on two fronts. On the one hand there was the project—a big enough task in itself—of challenging the canon of the great Australian tradition, itself barely a few decades old. This deconstructive enterprise had already begun in the work of feminist critics during the 1970s. It was therefore illuminating (and more than a little disheartening) to discover in this kindred territory institutionalised as Women's Studies a measure of hostility towards acknowledging principles of difference, in this case among women themselves. The second task involved the use of post-structuralist theory in a non-metropolitan, that is, Australian environment, which automatically involved further battles (Gunew, 1992).

Given these ferments, it has been useful to locate such debates within the formations of national cultures. Appropriate models are to be found in recent research into 'Englishness' and the rise of English studies in the UK, analysed as a moral technology complicit with structures of imperialism. As Terry Eagleton (1983) pointed out long ago, English literary studies functioned to produce depoliticised subjectivities. Current work on the Australian version of English studies and their significance in the Australian situation is progressing. To trace the impact of English studies on the rise of Australian studies would be a very useful exercise in deconstructing Australian culture.

Early in 1992 the first anthology of critical essays on multicultural literature was published under the title *Striking Chords: Multicultural Literary Interpretations* (Gunew and Longley, 1992b). This anthology contains up-to-date bibliographic information on critical studies in the area of Australian ethnic minority literatures. It includes a wide range of approaches, ranging from special-author studies to thematic approaches and those which use post-structuralist theoretical perspectives. The book also contains statements by writers on how they position themselves in the multicultural writing debates. Quite often, and rightly so given their current conditions, writers object to the special pleading they perceive as inherent in the label 'ethnic' or 'multicultural' writer. Understandably, they wish to be considered as Australian writers. When they describe themselves in those terms, they assume that their ethnicity is accepted as part of that designation, whereas this is still not the case when used in the wider community. Illuminating comparisons may be made with statements by writers in Hutcheon and Richmond (1990).

Publishing/editing/reviewing

To bring forward these issues into the public cultural arena still results in major battles. It remains important, however, to make these challenges in mainstream contexts rather than always in special-interest journals. This work of intervention in mainstream journals is a central part of the enterprise, for it questions those assumptions which permeate current constructions of the national culture. It is crucial that people stop seeing such perspectives as those of a minuscule minority, for the next generation will be bristling with them. There will be no further need then for these relatively crude strategies.

The 'literature machine' has many components, at each of which interventions need to be made, whether by editing new anthologies, publishing essays, or contributing to conferences and professional gatherings. The work is spread over a wide arena, and is very dependent on intersecting networks of patronage (Gunew, Papastergiadis and Blonski, 1994a). A key component is the relatively small scale of publishing in Australia, which has always made things difficult for marginal writers. However, the rise of small publishers as a result of desktop publishing is encouraging. Some of these have links to ethnic communities, but others do not. Literature, like many other art-forms, is not simply an extension of or coterminous with any community, ethnic or otherwise. A related consideration is that as yet there has been no systematic attempt to assess the role of ethnic media either in giving a forum to ethnic minority writers or in airing cultural matters to both minority and majority audiences.

Policy work

In recent years, the work of Tony Bennett (1992a, 1992b), Stuart Cunningham (1992) and Ian Hunter (Hunter et al., 1991) in the

Institute for Cultural Policy Studies at Griffith University in Queensland has alerted us to the importance of theorising policy work in relation to studies in the humanities. My own experience of such matters emerges from a different position, namely of how policy is formulated in a number of state institutions. For three years I was a Council Member of the Australia Council, and I have also been on the federal Cultural Heritage Advisory Committee as well as the Multicultural Advisory Committee for the Victorian Ministry for the Arts. All of these appointments involved formulating policy on multicultural cultural matters. As a consequence I am less optimistic than some are about the ability of academics, acting as consultants on policy, to maintain an uncompromising critical distance in such work. Like my colleagues at Griffith University, however, I am convinced that in this area there needs to be as much intellectual debate on and engagement with the issues as possible. The role of those co-opted on to a variety of federal and State committees which deal with the formation of policy for managing the cultural sphere is a troubled one. To be regarded as the repository of all things relating to multicultural matters, for example, is a highly problematic activity. The first step consists of always making sure that one is connected to the 'field' outside in order to be able to act as a conduit for disseminating information in both directions. Consider two such examples.

The Australia Council is a federal body that controls funding in the subsidised arts, which currently make up around 6 per cent of all cultural funding. Though this seems a small and elitist area, its symbolic stature cannot be underestimated. In the last decade various attempts have been made to formulate policy guidelines for bringing non-English-speaking background (NESB) artists into the arts-funding arena. It is not that they haven't been producing art; the problem is that their work is neither given the kind of support it deserves nor recognised as part of the national culture. The Australia Council, in response to the *National Agenda on Multiculturalism* (1989), has developed a Council-wide 'Arts for a Multicultural Australia' policy (see Blonski, 1992), which is a series of strategies for both encouraging and coping with the processing of applications from NESB artists. One problem is that these are still seen too often as falling automatically within community arts business, together with what are deemed working-class or community artists in general. This aspect of the arts-funding area is animated by principles of access and equity that by current definitions are incompatible with those questions of aesthetic judgement or 'excellence' in the arts which the Australia Council defines as its major mission. In other words, excellence is usually defined as transcending such socio-political categories as class or gender or ethnicity. This means that the kind of informed professionalism which operates in adjudicating funding in the major art-form panels does not function in the same way within the community arts. Here an unproblematic concept of the 'community' dominates in relation to class, gender and cultural diversity. In this context individual artists of non-Anglo-Celtic backgrounds who do not see themselves as community artists have a tough time.

In 1991 the Cultural Heritage Advisory Committee was convened to draft a plan for encouraging all the collecting institutions in the country—such as libraries, museums, art museums and archives—to respond to cultural diversity. This exercise represents the other side of the cultural coin. While the Australia Council distinguishes between heritage arts and contemporary arts and funds only the latter, the Cultural Heritage Advisory Committee addresses the nature of Australia's heritage. What do we choose to conserve and display, or, who 'owns' the past? Once again this has precipitated some interesting conceptual categories, mostly to do with 'heritage' itself, and has also thrown into relief what people mean when they respond to multiculturalism by saying that they will consult with and involve ethnic communities in their institutional practices. Who these communities are, and who is to represent them, become major concerns. Also noteworthy is the recognition that institutional managers rarely consider that the professionals they need may well be found in non-Anglo-Celtic areas, or even that their own current staff have culturally diverse skills to offer. In other words, the 'ethnics' continue to be seen as inhabiting a space 'out there' and not in here and part of 'us'. This in a nutshell is the multicultural dilemma in institutional and policy matters (Gunew and Rizvi, 1994b). But let us pause here and consider a little further the interplay between heritage, memory and history in relation to multiculturalism, and specifically the multilingual dimension of non-Anglo-Celtic Australia.

Reinventing the national culture

In the penultimate chapter of the revised version of his influential book *Imagined Communities*, Benedict Anderson makes the somewhat surprising point that rather than simply deriving their nationalisms from European dynastic states, colonial states may be said in fact to have structured the very grammar of nationalism. He consolidates this claim through an analysis of the census, the map and the museum. Using the methodology of totalising classification (the census and map), European usurpers constructed what Anderson (1991:174–5) terms a 'political-biographical narrative' of 'the property history of their new possessions'. Museums in turn encourage the museumisation of sacred sites as 'regalia for a secular state' (ibid.:182), their most important characteristic being their infinite reproducibility in postcards and books, etc. Nowadays we tend to refer to this process as 'cultural tourism'.

Clearly traced here is a relationship between structuring the genealogy of nationalism (a process equally as fraught in the post-colonial era as it was in colonial times), and who or what is both included and excluded by this activity. Nationalism is always linked to territory, and traditionally is predicated on genealogy, an imagined narrative of kinship and descent that Anderson calls 'serial continuity' (ibid.:195).

Since ethnic minorities are often signified through their 'other' languages, it is pertinent to ask here what role language plays in this transfer of ownership from one group to another. According to a recent study of community languages (Clyne, 1991), over sixty languages other than English are spoken in Australia. The relationship between nationalism, territory and language is an ambiguous one. As Anderson also points out, in the European states there was rarely a synonymity between territory and language users. However, in a particular formation or process of mythification, language is swiftly yoked to the nationalist enterprise. Thus arose, for example, the notion of the 'civilising' effects of certain languages. Not coincidentally, a hierarchical table of languages was structured entirely according to imperial expansions.

In the recent and expanding field devoted to the study of English and Englishness, numerous commentators link the construction of English as an academic study to a nationalist moral technology, in which Englishness functions both internally (to civilise the working class, for example) and externally to unify the Empire. English literature was disseminated as a civilising force because it was seen to be less compromising politically than Christianity, as Gauri Viswanathan (1989) has shown. Another analyst, Brian Doyle (1989), points out the ways in which English was first constructed out of thoroughly un-native antecedents and then, by a dazzling sleight of hand, turned into a natural and quintessentially native language. Doyle also suggests that the study of English literature, especially nowadays, 'involves a retreat into a museum-like or "monumental" role with teachers of English as professional curators of a residual "national cultural heritage"' (Doyle, 1989:135). Thus in this era of burgeoning literatures in English, English literature still functions as the legitimate and legitimising origins of the language, wherever it operates. English holds the spectre of the old empire together. For proof one need only mention those apoplectic newspaper letters provoked by the release of language policies which attempt to capitalise on Australia's linguistic diversity. Like the Union Jack, the English language itself is a guarantee of the mother country, a sign that one has been born as a legitimate descendant.

What is the relationship of these 'other' languages (and their attendant literatures and cultural traditions) to the diasporic phenomenon in which they are enmeshed? Clearly, and this has been much analysed, there are numerous contradictions and tensions between a so-called genuine or original form of a language and its bastard offsprings developed far from home. Some have argued the reverse, of course, namely that the genuine article has in fact been preserved by being exported, and that purer versions of a language (and culture) now prevail within the diasporic phenomenon.

How do these languages function in Australia? They operate

differently according to their institutional embedding, that is, according to whether they are taught in tertiary language departments across Australia, or whether they are closely tied to local communities in those 'Saturday' or other schools which have responded to their constituents' pressures to maintain such languages. That the teaching of languages is tied to various kinds of cultural maintenance is also often the case, and once again such elements are shaped by whether such classes are located in mainstream educational institutions or in community ones.[4] Given the class patterns of migration in Australia, there are both high-culture and low-culture types of linguistic diversity. The high-culture version is to be found in tertiary language departments not necessarily interested in the diasporic phenomenon; whereas in the popular and low-culture developments we encounter community languages which are linked inevitably to manifestations of diaspora. A third suggestion, acknowledging the diasporic experience, is that these languages develop within the new context their own complex histories of representation and hybrid textualities. One aspect of this has been dubbed 'multicultural literature', which is a globalised manifestation of the local in writing.

The question remains as to how this phenomenon should be managed in heritage terms. In the federal heritage plan released in Australia a few years ago, collecting institutions were encouraged to consult with those local communities who comprise their immediate catchment areas. Museums, libraries and art museums were asked to acknowledge cultural diversity by interacting with such communities. But what exactly is 'the community' in this model? In an article exploring that very term, the American philosopher Iris Young critiques prevailing concepts of 'community' which are organised around the metaphysics of presence and an identity politics:

> The ideal of community participates in what Derrida calls the metaphysics of presence and Adorno calls the logic of identity, a metaphysics that denies difference. The ideal of community presumes subjects can understand one another as they understand themselves. It thus denies the difference between sub-

jects. The desire for community relies on the same desire for social wholeness and identification that underlies racism and ethnic chauvinism on the one hand and political sectarianism on the other . . . setting up an opposition between authentic and inauthentic social relations . . . Any move to define an identity, a closed totality, always depends on excluding some elements, separating the pure from the impure. (Young, 1990:302)

The notion of community she puts forward is framed instead by a model of the city as the tolerant juxtaposition of various groups— an openness, as she calls it, to 'unassimilated otherness' (ibid.:319). The will to eradicate otherness exists in the current treatment of language groups in Australia. Elsewhere I have analysed this phenomenon in terms of the pure and the impure, and most recently in relation to the concept of 'abjection' developed by Julia Kristeva (Gunew, 1993b).

Further to this point, Anna Yeatman (1994) distinguishes two kinds of relationships between state and community, which she designates the 'customary' and the 'conventionalist'. The customary relationship is based on a model of genealogy and kinship and involves a common language and a common culture. The conventionalist relationship, on the other hand, responds to challenges offered by feminism, post-colonialism and multiculturalism: it is based on acceptance of legal structures that allow different groups to operate together, and with commonly held values which guarantee equal access to resources by all groups, whether such resources are symbolic or other kinds of capital. Like Young's thesis, Yeatman's is built around a politics of difference. In brief, a national heritage which accommodates different languages can survive only in a society based on conventionalist rather than customary principles.

Thus diasporic languages and cultures serve to deconstruct a nationalism based on those exclusive imaginaries which are structured around heritage in terms of kinship and genealogy, common descent and language. Such matters are not dealt with adequately by speaking to or appointing some of those self-styled community spokespeople encountered in ethnic political networks. It is far more significant to scrutinise the ways in which the writings of

these different language groups deconstruct that spuriously unified national culture whose 'unity' is based, as Young suggests, on
the eradication of the very difference it supposedly avows. This
point is developed at greater length in a recent book by Floya
Anthias and Nira Yuval-Davis (1992) discussed in the next chapter. Their contention is that, as a plan for managing cultural
diversity, multicultural policy constructs communities in terms of
an ethnic absolutism which results in separate and homogeneous
entities. Within a social justice framework, participation by the
community is often further reduced to those activists who speak
on its behalf. In turn, the community comes to signify a motley
collection of outsiders. Where the artist is concerned, it has rightly
been pointed out that the creative individual is often at odds with
the concept of community (Anthias and Yuval-Davis, 1992:158).
Much of this is pertinent to the Australian context. How can we
ensure that these differences operate *specifically* within Australian culture, and in terms that will not construct them as mere
addenda to the dominant culture? It is precisely in the multicultural
arena that we encounter most confusion between the two ways of
defining 'culture': first as those many elements which symbolically organise life, such as food, language, religion, and rite-of-
passage ceremonies; and second as artistic productions which
constitute culture in the sense of art or high culture. Multiculturalism in Australia is acceptable as a celebration of costumes,
customs and cooking. It is not acceptable as high culture.

Redefining the public sphere

The moment they move away from social or welfare issues, those
working in the multicultural field in Australia find that they are still
talking mainly among themselves. Multiculturalism continues to
be reduced to 'the migrant condition'. Thus the reception of
multicultural writings in Australia (even those written in English)
swings between primitivism (or nativism) and Eurocentrism—the
endorsement being offered in both cases by emissaries from the
'civilised' centre. Needless to say, there are hierarchies of languages and cultures within Australia. And while Australia can
cope to some extent with both the North (France and Germany)

and the South (Italy and Greece), it begins to have problems the moment it confronts the East or non-West.

The very term, 'multicultural literature', already conjures up the spectre of homogenisation. What are the common points, except perhaps certain thematic preoccupations, between an Italo-Australian and a Vietnamese-Australian text? The thematic concerns most favoured by editors, publishers, and reviewers tend to be those which deal overtly with the migrant experience, and preferably in the generic form of confessional oral history. This results in a couple of related problems: reductive homogenisation, and 'representation' by tokenism.

In order to block such moves in the treatment of multicultural literature, a few scholars have attempted to develop the strategies outlined above. In particular, they have set up 'cultural difference' as a category within cultural analysis, so that critics will not always rediscover the same, but allow instead for those incommensurable differences which resist assimilation. This includes allowing also for the heterogeneity not only of different languages but also of that which exists within each language. Non-Anglo-Celts need not always speak either in the first person or about the migrant experience; they too may play about the edges of English and other languages.

Nor can such issues and contradictions be resolved by finding the right terminology for these writings. Simply to call them 'migrant writing' often amounts to maintaining a reductive notion of their content (they deal 'simply' with the migrant experience) and locating them in oral history and sociology, where they signify 'migrant problems'. To describe them as 'non-Anglo-Celtic writing' is both to define them negatively and to generate unnecessary controversy about their relation to older settler groups in Australia. To call them 'multicultural writing' is to homogenise the very differences which are demanding to be analysed. In this study I have settled for 'ethnic minority writing', partly because it signals that such writing needs to be seen always in relation to something designated (although rarely in any overt manner) as ethnic *majority* writing; this usage ensures that cultural majority groups no longer remain invisible. The term 'ethnic minority writing' also encourages the analysis of cultural difference as a critical category within cultural criticism. In the next chapter I shall examine, among other matters, the complexities of ethnicity. None of these terms is satisfactory because all present problems. We also need to consider the terms in which these minority writings are discussed within a global context, because ultimately the global dimension is a significant factor in all these debates, although this has not been recognised generally in Australia. Speaking pragmatically, we have to make sure that these writings are preserved, and that their extent and diversity are acknowledged in the various classifications and taxonomies to be found in national cultural institutions. We also need to foment as much debate as possible concerning their significance.

In the remainder of this study, Part I examines the theoretical frameworks appropriate to multicultural literary studies. Chapter 2 summarises both the debt to post-colonial theory and the adjacent contributions from debates about the formation of national cultures, especially those concerning ethnicity and race. Chapter 3 looks at the kindred 'minority' area of feminist theory (and notably the work of Julia Kristeva), focusing in particular on that problem of 'authenticity' which often functions reductively in discussions of both women's writing and ethnic minority writings. Part II comprises readings of some major theorists of subjectivity (notably those who use psychoanalytic concepts) and writers who use the first person in non-realist and non-autobiographical ways. Chapter 4 analyses the poetry and poetic prose of Antigone Kefala and Ania Walwicz in relation to concepts of the literary and the avant-garde. Chapter 5 discusses the controversial work of Rosa Cappiello in the context of Bakhtin's theory of carnival. The final chapter examines in the urban and postmodernist work of Anna Couani the issue of the homeland and nostalgia, using as its point of entry Sigmund Freud's seminal essay 'The Uncanny'.

PART I

Framing Marginality

Marginal Positions: Constructing Cultural Differences on Various 'Posts'

Framing aesthetics

Being marginalised cannot be reduced simply to a struggle between oppressor and oppressed in which the latter remains utterly
passive. In their spatially conceived representation of exclusionary
gestures, margins have always been ambiguous signs which have
served to frame the centre in terms of indictment as well as
approbation. This point is raised in all its complexity in Derrida's
essay 'The Parergon', which examines the terrain of aesthetic
judgement by means of a reading of Immanuel Kant's *Critique of
Judgment*, by way of Martin Heidegger. After pondering the
nature of *parerga* (ornamentation), and specifically the drapery
surrounding statues, Derrida moves to consider the columns
adjacent to buildings, and from thence to the concept of the
border or frame. This process raises fundamental questions about
what is excluded and what included in the operation of aesthetic
judgement. First, how is the object defined in terms of its relevant
constituent elements, and then how is it evaluated? As Derrida
puts it:

> No 'theory', no 'practice', no 'theoretical practice' can be effec-
> tive here if it does not rest on the frame, the invisible limit of
> (between) the interiority of meaning (protected by the entire
> hermeneutic, semiotic, phenomenological, and formalist tradi-
> tion) *and* (of) all the extrinsic empiricals which, blind and

illiterate, dodge the question . . . Every analytic of aesthetic judgment presupposes that we can rigorously distinguish between the intrinsic and the extrinsic. (Derrida, 1979:24–6)

Later he refers to the 'violence of framing'. The rationale for this procedure is precisely the underlying logic of classic deconstruction, which posits that the elements excluded in the analytical process are the conditions of its possibilities. Thus the exclusions or marginalisation of certain writings in fact frame the conditions of existence of those *other* writings which are included or endorsed by the analytical process. 'Framing always sustains and contains that which, by itself, collapses forthwith' (ibid.:36). It is in this sense that 'ethnic minority writing' may be said to 'frame' Australian literature. The discussion of the frame may be seen as a variation on (or adjunct to) the concept of the supplement, which has proved helpful for those interested in theorising a legitimate place and role for marginalised or minority cultural productions. But it is necessary to move from this abstract metalevel to the particular, even though this means taking a route through the universal.

Universal culture

The question of a common cultural literacy for the Anglophone world is much debated in the US, UK, Canada and Australia. English has become the language not only of those who comprise but also of those who aspire to be part of the advanced capitalist world. Those in the market for buying English language teaching waver between the desirability of the American-accented or British-accented versions. The cultural embeddings of this language are a related issue. 'Will English survive without Shakespeare?' trumpet the daily papers whenever curriculum reform is being debated. Since the answer to this is obviously affirmative at one level, 'Shakespeare' clearly functions here as a signifier of English (in the sense of specifically British) civilisation.

But how does one begin to approach this question of a desirable cultural literacy, embedded as it is in assumptions about the cohesiveness of national cultures? What should every (English-speaking) child know? Can ex-Commonwealth countries like Australia afford to dilute the British cultural legacy with those other cultural traditions which inform the backgrounds of one in four, or even one in three, of the Australian population? Will this allow them to have the same chances in later life, and equip them for the tough economic struggle which lies ahead? It may be that this is a spurious way of putting it, but consider the following questions. Why and when are certain cultures given a universal status, and what are the implications of this, for themselves and for other cultures? To what extent can we make room for competing cultures within a national framework? How can we represent the cultural difference of the 'other' without appropriating it?

Civilised (male) subjects

> the history of the concept of man is never questioned. Everything takes place as though the sign 'man' has no origin, no historical, cultural, linguistic limit, not even a mctaphysical limit. (Derrida,1969:35)

The notion of 'universal man' has received such a battering in the latter half of this century that we cannot invoke it quite so easily as pundits in previous eras used to do (Eagleton, 1991). The concept of a transcendent and unified human subject as the origin of meaning dates back to René Descartes ('I think therefore I am') and the Enlightenment (Grosz, 1990; Rothfield, 1990). Furthermore, in the last few decades philosophers such as Jean-François Lyotard (1984) have defined our current episteme, the postmodern, in terms of a loss of faith in metanarratives. Such developments come in the wake of Jacques Derrida's demonstration that western epistemology is based on a metaphysics of presence and a logocentrism in which writing is privileged over speech (see Norris, 1982).

In other words, in the last two decades or so certain frames that represent dominant ways of thought have been made visible. The corollary is that the same process has exposed those elements hitherto excluded or on the margins, and whose existence makes possible both the dominant and the norm. Feminism's analyses of patriarchy were among the first to take advantage of this new turn in philosophy. In Genevieve Lloyd's work, for instance, the concept of reason itself is revealed to be predicated on a masculinist model (Lloyd,1984; see also Grosz, 1989; Jardine, 1985). The critique of White dominance by critics involved in Black studies (Dyer, 1988) is a further example of such critiques. In Australia, analyses of the marginalisation of both Aboriginal and non-Anglo-Celtic Australians have also benefited from these new developments in philosophy. These varying interrogations of the 'standard' and the 'measure' have undermined the Enlightenment construction of the human subject as transcendent, fully conscious and rational (Belsey, 1985; Henriques, 1984).

One of the metanarratives targeted by Lyotard (1989) is that apparently paradoxical notion of the universal history of Western civilisation. This supposedly universal account, which is of course quite culturally specific, has provided the model for various narratives of national culture, including Australia's own. Paradoxically, and once again, certain specific national cultures are traditionally seen as emblematic of Western civilisation—France, the UK, and the US. It may not surprise us to note that they are all colonial powers. Indeed, one of the most productive areas of critical analysis in the last decade has been the examination of links between various allegedly transnational imperial projects and their very specific national starting-points (Said, 1993).

Edward Said, a Palestinian and Professor of English at Columbia University in New York, has significantly shaped contemporary debates around imperialism and culture. His own landmark work, *Orientalism* (1979), looks at the ways in which the 'Orient' exists primarily (perhaps even exclusively) as a projection and confirmation of the West, functioning to condone the West's treatment and exploitation of those diverse cultures it traditionally homogenises under this inadequate term. Said's study highlights the fact that representation itself—that crucially mediated way in which we construct and interpret reality—always contains a kind of violence, in the sense that it involves selections and exclusions which are carried out from certain positions and perspectives whose operations are usually rendered invisible:

Certainly representation, or more particularly the *act* of representing (and hence reducing) others, almost always involves a violence of some sort to the *subject* of representation, as well as a contrast between the violence of the act of representing something and the calm exterior of the representation itself, the *image*—verbal, visual, or otherwise—of the subject . . . What we must eliminate are systems of representation that carry with them the kind of authority which . . . has been repressive because it doesn't permit or make room for interventions on the part of those represented. (Said, 1990: 94–5)

Thus the fictions or narratives with which we make sense of the world are subject to all the contradictory codes inherent in textuality. This is not to argue that there is no reality outside textuality, but merely to point out that many of our perceptions come to us 'textualised' as representations in some form or other. When considering the central role of representation, it is useful to recall that we use the term in at least two senses: representation as 'depiction' and representation as 'delegation', that is, when someone represents a group or an individual (Spivak, 1988:276; Julien and Mercer, 1988:4). Increasingly over the last two decades, critics who are delegates for marginal or minority groups have attempted to focus on those hitherto invisible lineaments of the West, namely Western metaphysics and material practices. 'The hegemony implicit in the phrase, "the Western tradition"', notes Henry Louis Gates Jr (1987:32), 'primarily reflects material relationships, and not so-called universal, transcendent, normative judgments. Judgment is specific, both culturally and temporally'.

For instance, in analysing the attributes of the West as continuous with White hegemony, Richard Dyer (1988:45–7) describes the power of whiteness as its ability to be both no colour and all colours, so that it apparently avoids or transcends the typical, and comes to represent the full diversity of human experience. Those who represent whiteness, in both senses, are rarely seen as doing this. Developing further this concept of an invisible norm, Robert Young (1990:19) states that 'postmodernism can best be defined as European culture's awareness that it is no longer the unquestioned and dominant centre of the world'. Young's book anatomises the imbrication of White civilisation with concepts of universalism. The guiding question which informs both his own work and that of the critics he summarises is how to change this focus on 'white mythologies'. How do we represent other cultures in such a way as to avoid 'mastering' or appropriating them? A variety of answers is provided by Edward Said, Homi Bhabha, Gayatri Chakravorty Spivak and others whose work is described below.

The problem of representing (in both senses) alterity has dominated post-structuralist and postmodernist thought, particularly in relation to political agendas. In this respect it is useful to note Homi Bhabha's comments on an often invoked binary opposition, the relation of theoretical to political practices:

> The function of theory within the political process becomes two-edged. It makes us aware that our political referents and priorities—the people, the community, class struggle, anti-racism, gender difference, the assertion of an anti-imperialist, black or third-world perspective—are not 'there' in some primordial naturalistic sense. Nor do they reflect a unitary or homogeneous political object. (Bhabha, 1988:11)

Alterity

In order to relativise the universalist tendency to assume centrist positions of power and truth, how can we accommodate difference without appropriating the 'other', whether that other is female or someone from a non-Western or non-English-speaking culture (bearing in mind that these terms too are highly reductive)? Recent emancipatory movements are characterised by their frequent references to the 'other', as in relations of women to men, Blacks to Whites, or working class to middle class. What is noticeable is that this oft-invoked 'other' usually occupies a subjugated position. Even (or perhaps particularly) those intellectual endeavours which purport to analyse and deconstruct such relations are often predicated in fact on their maintenance. The impulse toward mastery, the nexus between knowledge and power, is a sustaining one (Foucault, 1979, 1980).

A disciplinary area where this is most easily exemplified is anthropology, which is traditionally the place in which one culture is scrutinised and summed up by another. Recently, post-structuralist upheavals have occurred in this discipline also, and critics such as James Clifford articulate the problem of alterity and ethnocentrism succinctly in the statement, 'we have history, they have myth' (Clifford et al., 1987:125). Abdul JanMohammed and David Lloyd point out that 'minority individuals are always treated and forced to experience themselves generically' (JanMohammed and Lloyd, 1987:10), that is, they are excluded automatically from claiming universality (see also Trinh, 1989; Chow, 1989:161). Gayatri Spivak (1990) offers a sustained analysis of the many ways in which, by this process, the all-knowing analyst remains supposedly neutral and invisible, and therefore in a position of immense power. This point is echoed by Nancy Hartsock (1987:195): 'the creation of the Other is simultaneously the creation of the transcendent and omnipotent theoriser who can persuade himself that he exists outside time and space and power relations'. Here is a terse statement of what it means to exist as other:

> But can you even imagine what it is to live in a culture, and live as one of that culture, which owes nothing to, say, Christendom and Christian ethics and the history and legends and traditions of Western civilization? Imagine rethinking all your language and all your exchanges and encounters, all your greetings and your jokes and your insults. And above all imagine *having* to do this, having to do this in the face of the arrogance of a culture which has not only ruled much of the world but also finds it inconceivable that a culture formerly its subject and slave might possess anything even resembling knowledge, let alone wisdom. (Sivaramakrishnan, 1989:6)

Literary criticism forms part of this analytical hegemony, which is analysed by Edward Said (1984a) as following two trajectories: the sacred and the secular. The sacred seeks to fill the gap left by the decline of religion in the modernist era, in the traditional sense that we have models of truth sustained by acts of faith. We have erected, says Said, a new 'religiosity in criticism', a class of priests promulgating a sacred language which excludes non-initiates. It also excludes an awareness of the specific historical and material conditions which produce certain texts and certain readings; in other words, the process involved in interpretation becomes transparently an act of faith accepted by the congregation of readers. Such 'expertise is therefore supposed to be unaffected by its institutional affiliations with power' (Said, 1983:152; see also Said, 1987:140–1).

In *Orientalism* Said (1979) exemplifies the other trajectory, secular criticism, when he traces the history of a sustained construction of otherness (see particularly ch. 1). About a decade later he reformulated his project in this study as being not

> a defense either of the Arabs or of Islam—as my book was taken by many to be—my argument was that neither existed except as 'communities of interpretation' which gave them existence, and that, like the Orient itself, each designation represented interests, claims, projects, ambitions and rhetorics that were not only in violent disagreement, but were in a situation of open warfare. So saturated with meanings, so overdetermined by history, religion and politics are labels like 'Arab' or 'Muslim' as subdivisions of 'The Orient' that no one today can use them without some attention to the formidable polemical mediations that screen the objects, if they exist at all, that the labels designate . . . The Orient was therefore not Europe's interlocutor, but its silent Other. (Said,1985:16–17)

Now, in the wake of this study, the 'Orient' and the culturally marginalised the world over have indeed become the interlocutors of the West, as exemplified in the title of a recent study in postcolonial literature, *The Empire Writes Back* (Ashcroft, Griffiths and Tiffin,1989).[1]

Following Said's endeavours, Homi Bhabha departs from his precursor and to some degree provides a critique of aspects of Said's work, notably in relation to the over-simplification of the supposed binary opposition between coloniser and colonised (Young, 1990:ch. 8). This has implications for the question of locating agency in bringing about social change. In other words, what is the nexus between critical analysis and social change? According to Robert Young's critique, Bhabha himself does not answer this in terms of an easily apprehended politics of change;

that is, his readings of the texts of colonialism (particularly those related to India) reveal their covert subversions but do not make clear how or when these were examples or acts of rebellion. Put another way, how do they differ from other deconstructive or psychoanalytic readings which function to unravel any text?

Using psychoanalytic techniques of textual interpretation, particularly in his early essays, Bhabha concentrates on undoing the monological and unisonant authority of colonial discourse. Assuming as the basis of its power that it can fully define knowledge, it produces 'otherness' as stereotypes or the fixing of difference; and its implication in psychoanalytic economies of fantasy and desire is illustrated by an emphasis on that 'scopic' drive which reproduces the colonised as the object of the colonising gaze, 'the look'. For example, writing of Fanon's importance in the critique of colonialism, Bhabha states: 'The black presence ruins the representative narrative of Western personhood . . . The white man's eyes break up the black man's body and in the act of epistemic violence its own frame of reference is transgressed, its field of vision disturbed' (1990c:185). Stereotypes are seen here not simply as false images but as a process of constituting difference as though it were transfixed and paralysed by full knowledge:

> The objective of colonial discourse is to construe the colonised as a population of degenerate types on the basis of racial origin, in order to justify conquest and to establish systems of administration and instruction . . . colonial discourse produces the colonised as a fixed reality which is at once an 'other' and yet entirely knowable and visible. (Bhabha, 1983b:23, 33)

In sum, colonial discourse is 'one powerful nation writing out another' (Bhabha, 1985b:74), a movement back and forth between visibility and invisibility. There is no simple division here into a binary opposition between coloniser and colonised—the two are locked into each other:

> The Nationalist critic, caught in the problematic of image analysis, speaks against one stereotype but essentially, and inevitably, for another. The static nature of 'stereotype-analysis'—which is the image caught outside the process of the text—demands that the derogatory stereotype must be replaced

by positive ('Nationalist') images, which oppose the *undif-ferentiating* liberal humanist discourse of Universalism . . . In shattering the mirror of representation, and its range of Western bourgeois social and psychological 'identifications', the specta-cle of colonial fantasy sets itself up as an 'uncanny' double. (Bhabha, 1984a:105, 119)

Just as post-colonial history in general takes place in a scheme adjacent to 'universal' history, so the post-colonial moment, ar-gues Bhabha, is caught in a different time-scheme from that which governs the metropolitan centre; there is always a time-lag in-volved. This in turn leads post-colonial subjects to perform their inevitable exclusion from humanist discourses in repetitive stag-ings or performances that mark the process. In opening up modernity to post-colonial translations, one needs to look for the *petits récits* (those 'minor narratives' as distinct from the *grands récits* analysed by Lyotard) as well as for supplementary sites, moments and events.

Another critic often associated with Said and Bhabha in the post-colonial enterprise is Gayatri Chakravorty Spivak. Her con-cept of the 'native informant' as the 'self-confirming other' of Western civilisation (1988:284) provides a further perspective on the problem of alterity. Spivak (1983, 1986, 1987) also tackles, in ways that neither Said nor Bhabha does, the question of sexual difference as a crucial element in these positionings. Spivak came to fame as the translator of Derrida's *Of Grammatology* (1974), and continues to focus on Derrida's political significance in the face of critiques that deconstruction is somehow intrinsically apolitical. Always careful to analyse her own project and her own positioning, she might be described as offering a mixture of feminism, deconstruction and Marxism.

National cultures: Englishness/English studies

But what happens when we move from the wide-angled perspec-tive of imperialism to a focus on the national? Edward Said has defined nationalism in the following way:

Nationalism is an assertion of belonging in and to a place, a people, a heritage. It affirms the home created by a community of language, culture and customs; and, by so doing, it fends off exile, fights to prevent its ravages. Indeed, the interplay between nationalism and exile is like Hegel's dialectic of servant and master, opposites informing and constituting each other. All nationalisms in their early stages develop from a condition of estrangement. The struggles to win American independence, to unify Germany or Italy, to liberate Algeria were those of national groups separated—exiled—from what was construed to be their rightful way of life. Triumphant, achieved nationalism then justifies, retrospectively as well as prospectively, a history selectively strung together in a narrative form: thus all nationalisms have their founding fathers, their basic, quasi-religious texts, their rhetoric of belonging, their historical and geographical landmarks, their official enemies and heroes. This collective ethos forms what Pierre Bourdieu, the French sociologist, calls the *habitus*, the coherent amalgam of practices linking habit with inhabitance. (Said, 1984b:162)

Another recent critic, already mentioned, who has been influential in setting up the ways in which we read the story of a culture, of a nation, is Benedict Anderson.

All the great classical communities conceived of themselves as cosmically central, through the medium of a sacred language linked to a superterrestial order of power . . . In fact the deader the written language—the farther it was from speech—the better: in principle everyone has access to a pure world of signs. (Anderson, 1991:13)

Anderson develops a concept of 'imagined communities' as ways of organising a national culture on various levels. This has influenced the analysis of English studies in relation to Englishness, in various parts of the Anglophone world.[2] Also relevant here is Eric Hobsbawm's notion of an 'invented tradition', defined as 'a set of practices, normally governed by overtly or tacitly accepted rules and of a ritual or symbolic nature, which seek to inculcate certain values and norms of behaviour by repetition, which automatically implies continuity with the past' (Hobsbawm and Ranger, 1983:1).

An apt illustration of the invention of tradition is described in *The Function of Criticism* (1984), where Terry Eagleton traces the development during the eighteenth century of a 'public sphere' in which the bourgeoisie established themselves in opposition to the aristocratic state as an assembly marked by a civilised consensus exemplified in such journals as the *Tatler* and the *Spectator*. In the wake of the decline, this century, of this lucid and participatory model of analysis and debate, Eagleton argues that it is necessary to construct a counter-public sphere in which the role of the critic should be that of 're-connecting the symbolic to the political'. The public sphere comprises a series of discursive formations which legitimise and institutionally endorse a set of cultural practices. A counter-public sphere, on the other hand, qualifies and interrogates such authorisations by means of rational critique. An example of such a counter-public sphere, Eagleton suggests, is the women's movement. The Australian critic Andrew Milner (1985), drawing on the work of both Perry Anderson and Ben Anderson, as well as Eagleton, suggests that in Australia one of the totalising discourses of the public sphere has been located in history rather than in Leavisite literary criticism, which is what Perry Anderson (1968) had argued with respect to England. But let us consider further the nature and implications of public and counter-public spheres.

Post-colonial critiques

Edward Said (1984b:159) has suggested that 'modern Western culture is in large part the work of exiles, émigrés, refugees': in other words, it is the work of those who are separated implicitly from a notional public sphere. From this starting-point Said, in contrast to Eagleton, develops the notion of the critic as an exile imbued with 'contrapuntal' awareness, a term he borrows from music to indicate a productive tension resulting from a type of double vision. In an interview two years later, Said (1986) sets up this kind of critic in opposition to that theological mode of criticism discussed above. The critic as exile exemplifies a concept of criticism based on geography rather than history; it is a matter of overlapping and contested terrains rather than the search for a sacred originating point.

The development of post-colonialism has enabled those who are not part of the dominant and universalising culture to occupy a space from which to interrogate that very concept, and to put in its place a relativism in which cultural difference points to those varieties of subject-position which are part of all textual production. For example, Gayatri Spivak has formulated the concept of 'regulative psychobiographies'. By this she refers to those

> model narratives that give 'meaning' to our readings of ourselves and others. We are used to working with variations on, critiques of, and substitutions for, the narratives of Oedipus and Adam. What narratives produce the signifiers of the subject for other traditions? Always in a confrontation and complicity with the epistemic re-constitution of the subject-in-imperialism, traces of this psycho-biography can be found in the indigenous legal tradition, in the scriptures, and, of course, in myth. (Spivak, 1989a: 227)

She traces such psychobiographies in her work on suicide/sati (Spivak, 1985; 1988; see also Mani, 1985). Spivak distinguishes between post-colonialism and neo-colonialism as a way of drawing attention to the fact that colonialism is still operating, since the advanced capitalist nations quite clearly continue to exploit the Third World materially. This exploitation is supported by various regimes of representation and interpretation that constitute what she calls 'worlding' (Spivak, 1985, 1986, 1990; see also her analyses of the subaltern, 1987:ch. 12, and 1988).

Another strategy within post-colonialism has been to develop the concept of cultural difference alongside more familiar analytical categories such as class and gender. Spivak (1987:254) does this when she states that 'knowledge is made possible and sustained by irreducible difference, not identity', and again when she develops the notion (derived from Derrida) of the 'complete other' as distinct from the 'self-confirming other' (Spivak, 1988; see also Trinh, 1989:28ff.). Homi Bhabha has also been particularly useful in developing this concept of cultural difference, notably in relation to the difficulties of extricating such a critical category from its complicity with prevailing power structures:

> In order to be institutionally effective as a discipline, the knowledge of cultural difference must be made to foreclose on the Other; the 'Other' thus becomes at once the 'fantasy' of a

certain cultural space or, indeed, the certainty of a form of theoretical knowledge that deconstructs the epistemological 'edge' of the West. More significantly, the site of cultural difference becomes the mere phantom of a dire disciplinary struggle in which it has no space or power . . . However impeccably the content of an 'other' culture may be known, however anti-ethnocentrically it is represented, it is its *location* as the 'closure' of grand theories, the demand that, in analytical terms, it be always the 'good' object of knowledge, the docile body of difference, that reproduces a relation of domination and is the most serious indictment of the institutional powers of literary theory. (Bhabha, 1988:16)

It is illuminating to examine further some of the other concepts Bhabha develops in relation to his larger project of mapping the parameters of cultural difference. Particularly influential have been his concepts of 'incommensurability', 'hybridity' (1990d:211, 1990a, 1991), 'mimicry', and what he terms 'sly civility' (1984b, 1985a, 1985b). For example, by looking at the discourses of civility emanating not simply from the West in general but from the British empire in particular, he illustrates the ways in which in various contexts 'God' is equated not invariably with Englishness (Bhabha, 1985a). In developing these concepts, Bhabha focuses not on binary oppositions but on what he calls 'hybridity' (ibid.:174ff.). This term avoids the mutually stabilising effect of binary representation; he does not see it as passively reflective of socio-political relations. Instead, 'hybridity' emphasises that representation both produces such relations and structures the potential for meaning (Bhabha, 1984a:100). Bhabha emphasises cultural difference instead of cultural diversity, because 'diversity' is a conservative concept: often it simply comprises that spectacle of the exotic (Bhabha, 1988) which is consumed by hegemonic power relations and sustains them. Cultural difference, on the other hand, incorporates and draws attention to incommensurabilities not only between but also within cultures—in other words, to their essential untranslatability.

Following in the footsteps of Said, Bhabha and Spivak comes Tim Brennan's study of Salman Rushdie (Brennan, 1989). Brennan

distinguishes usefully between the postmodernist writer (as categorised by dominant institutional structures) and what he calls
'Third-World cosmopolitans'. These are energetic exiles who use
some of the techniques associated with postmodernism, and
whose work functions as a constant critique of nationalist and
imperialist projects, thereby foregrounding their politics in ways
not always associated with adherents of postmodernism. Rushdie
himself is also highly articulate about his own position in these
debates, as is illustrated in his collection of essays (Rushdie, 1991).
He has become of course a prime example of the ways in which
cultural work is embedded inevitably in political contexts over
which the author has no automatic control.

Trinh T. Minh-ha, a Vietnamese cinematographer and academic
now resident in the US, has developed a related theory of post-
colonial difference. This emphasises the positioning of women in
these debates as well as questions related to oral story-telling,
which is usually accorded an inferior status in cultural hierarchies.
Other directions in recent studies have focused on the way in
which in the new era of advanced capitalism the Third World is
mined as much for its cultural as for its more obviously material
resources. As Barbara Harlow puts it, Western theory creates a
new international division of labour, 'whereby the cultural raw
materials are mined in the Third World and delivered to the
manufacturing and processing centers of the First World where
they are transformed into commodities consumed by an educated
elite' (Harlow, 1989:168; see also Kaplan, 1987). Said's warning
(1989:213) against the ways in which difference is ominously and
consistently transformed into a spectacle is worth recalling here.
So too is Kum-Kum Sangari's account of modernism as contempo-
raneous with the classification of various cultures as 'Third World'
(Sangari, 1987; for a critique of some of these theorists see Porter,
1983; Parry, 1987; and Young, 1990).

Minority cultures/literatures

While post-colonialism represents a clear example of cultural
criticism emanating in part from minority perspectives, it is not the
only one. Black studies is another such case: now fitting to some

extent into post-colonialism, it predates the general use of the term, and is not entirely subsumed by it. Another example is the feminist enterprise, which has also undergone many changes. Under the influence of recent post-colonial feminism of the sort exemplified by the work of Spivak and Trinh, feminism has also had to come to terms with versions of itself as an orthodoxy. It has had to deal with critiques emanating from minority groups of women, who have felt marginalised by what was seen initially by those who practised it as a powerful and unified criticism of hegemonic and centrist enterprises (Gunew 1990b; Gunew and Yeatman, 1993).

The term 'minority literatures' is usually associated with the work of Deleuze and Guattari (1986), and especially their study of Kafka who, as a Jew writing in Prague, is perceived as exemplifying the category. Summarising their work, David Lloyd characterises a minor literature in the following manner:

> Any definition of 'minor' writing is obliged to take into account its oppositional status vis-à-vis canonical or major literature . . . Deleuze and Guattari . . . differentiate a literature of minorities written in a 'minority' language from a minor literature which would be that of minorities composed in a major language. For 'minor literature' is so termed in relation to the major canon, and its characteristics are defined in opposition to those which define canonical writing. To enumerate them briefly . . . the characteristics of a minor literature would involve the questioning or destruction of the concepts of identity and identification, the rejection of representations of developing autonomy and authenticity, if not the very concept of development itself, and accordingly a profound suspicion of narratives of reconciliation and unification. (Lloyd, 1987:173)

Other theorists of minority perspectives have been quite critical of this work (Kaplan, 1987). The minority perspective involves, as Said also points out, not only the construction of a new or counter-canon, but also the question of how the current ones function (Said, 1986:8; cf. Spivak, 1987:ch. 10). Minority discourse is thus not simply an oppositional or counter-discourse: it also undoes the power of dominant discourses to represent themselves as universal.

As a result of the making of these distinctions, other theorists have responded by developing a variety of strategies. Stuart Hall (1987, 1990), for example, concentrates on the notion of 'positionality', and relates this to a careful redefinition of 'ethnicity'. The responsibility for cultural translation involves learning to listen rather than to speak, and learning to speak *to* rather than *for* others (Spivak, 1987:135). Here once again Bhabha's notion of alertness to the incommensurable within cultures is important: 'it is the articulation *through* incommensurability that structures all narratives of identification, and all acts of cultural translation' (Bhabha, 1990b:313–19; see also Bhabha 1988, 1990d). He describes the turning of boundaries into in-between spaces available for purposes of negotiation. This is not unlike what Said suggests when he privileges geography rather than history (or space rather than time). Bhabha also suggests that

> the marginal or 'minority' is not the space of a celebratory, or utopian, self-marginalization. It is a much more substantial intervention into those justifications of modernity—progress, homogeneity, cultural organicism, the deep nation, the long past—that rationalize the authoritarian, 'normalizing' tendencies within cultures in the name of the national interest or the ethnic prerogative. (Bhabha, 1990b:4)

Gayatri Spivak and other commentators on the positioning of post-colonial 'minority' women alert us to the need for what could now be called hegemonic or orthodox feminism to deconstruct its own authoritarian and racist assumptions (see Spivak, 1987:ch. 12; Carby, 1982, 1986; Mohanty, 1988; Trinh, 1989). As Trinh puts it in relation to the dilemma faced by 'women of colour': 'The precarious line we walk on is one that allows us to challenge the West as authoritative subject of feminist knowledge, while also resisting the terms of binarist discourse that would concede feminism to the West all over again' (Trinh, 1992:153, 140). Like Spivak (1987:107, 1989b), Trinh (1989, 1992) also points constantly to the dangers of tokenism, which occurs when certain spokespeople for the marginal are consistently singled out as fully representative of those constituencies.

In the US and the UK as well as in Africa, Black culture, in its many manifestations, has been theorised in a variety of ways.

Stuart Hall has used this example to make more general points about the crucial factor of positionality in all constructions of subjectivity. 'The term ethnicity', he writes, 'acknowledges the place of history, language and culture in the construction of subjectivity and identity, as well as the fact that all discourse is placed, positioned, situated, and all knowledge is contextual' (Hall, 1988a: 29).[3]

Situated knowledge: the local

Current emphases on the 'local' (or the politics of location) are in some ways a logical development in the move away from universalism. To a certain extent, this emphasis has existed in feminism for some time; Teresa de Lauretis (1984), for example, defines 'experience' in such a way that it is not perceived as being in opposition to theory. Recent writings on the body and corporeality are another version of this trajectory (Grosz, 1994). However, the two essays which are directly relevant to location in the wake of post-colonialism are those by Rich (1986) and Haraway (1991:ch. 8). In a characteristically stringent reassessment of her earlier theories and practices, Adrienne Rich analyses the tendency towards abstraction and universalising that in the past had characterised both her own work and that of other white feminist theorists.

Haraway's essay is a complex analysis that places feminism in relation to what she calls 'situated knowledge', which is characteristic of all knowledge, although it does not proclaim itself in such terms. She deals with the discourses of science, which traditionally have laid claim to a defining objectivity. Haraway proves that this is as false as any other such claims to universalism, and critiques the argument often advanced to counter this move, namely that a departure from objectivity will simply land one in rampant relativism:

> the alternative to relativism is not totalization and single vision, which is always finally the unmarked category whose power depends on systematic narrowing and obscuring. The alternative to relativism is partial, locatable, critical knowledges sus-

taining the possibility of webs of connections called solidarity in politics and shared conversations in epistemology. (Haraway, 1991:191)

This is similar to Trinh's argument (1992) that the fragment is not necessarily defined exclusively as part of a whole. Haraway's essay ends with the crucial comment that the object of such situated knowledge needs to be seen as an actor and agent rather than as the the victim paralysed by the all-knowing look (Haraway 1991:198; cf. Bhabha, discussed above, on the power of 'the look' in colonialism).

Taking a slightly different line on the local (or located) knowledges and knowers, Stuart Hall has written a series of important studies (1988a, 1988b, 1988c) which define latter-day multinational capital as having appropriated the desire for ethnic diversity. In other words, ethnicity has been progressively commodified by a flexible capitalism able to cater for all tastes and to target numerous specialised consumer groups. The prevalence of ethnic diversity, however, is no guarantee of a new political awareness; on the contrary, ethnicity and difference are translated into both spectacle and depoliticised aesthetics as the 'exotic accessory'. Hall (1989) argues for a new concept of identity as process rather than fact, and the need to position oneself both inside and outside certain systems of representation. Although such systems are inescapable, it is possible to use these positions strategically. Referring to Derrida's concept of *différance* as encompassing both 'difference' and 'deferral', Hall remarks that this does not mean that because there can be no permanent positioning there can be no meaning, but rather that because positioning is always temporary, meanings are always provisional. The importance lies in always recognising the role of history and the prevailing circumstances of power :

Far from being grounded in a necessary 'recovery' of the past, which is waiting to be found, and which, when found, will secure our sense of ourselves into eternity, identities are the names we give to the different ways we are positioned by, and position ourselves within, the narratives of the past. (Hall 1989:70)

In the long run, to 'situate' knowledge in this way is to acknowl-edge the need for accountability in all our theorising and research endeavours (see also Said, 1984a:226–47, and the comments on this essay by Clifford [1989]). To discover ways of addressing such local manifestations is part of the enterprise of multicultural critical theory.

Multiculturalism: between ethnicity and race

Multiculturalism, as noted, is a term with global resonances but very different national inflections. In the UK and the US (and to a lesser extent Canada and New Zealand) it has become a coded way of addressing issues to do with race. It amounts to recognising and managing the heterogeneous composition of modern nation-states, and devising ways of addressing it in relation to cultural literacy. But even this formulation is of course far too general.

In Australia there has not been the same emphasis on race. This is because questions of cultural difference have been played out within a Western and largely European framework, where the difference appears to be between Anglo-Celtic and non-Anglo-Celtic languages and cultural traditions. In other words, the inevi-tability of having to deal with heterogeneity in the wake of postwar migrations was on the whole confined to those large groups comprising Mediterranean or southern Europeans, mainly from Italy and Greece. Although there are histories of these groups having been treated in racial terms, they were not signifi-cant in the long run. In the wake of later and so-called Asian migrations, race increasingly became both a covert and an overt factor, and debates on immigration in the Australian context became a coded way of addressing 'racial' differences perceived as more challenging than 'ethnic' differences.

But increasingly the movement between race and ethnicity has merged in the global context. In some ways these Australian distinctions, born out of the historical accidents of migration, offer a way of dealing with the current state of such debates as they have emerged elsewhere. Increasingly one could say that the over-simplified categories of race have been retrieved or rehabilitated for the purposes of more precise analyses by becoming 'ethnicised'.

Thus the old opposition of Black versus White has been broken down, and not before time, into their differences. For example, it has been pointed out that although racism may often be signified in terms of Black victims, this does not offer any causal explanation for the details of discrimination (Anthias and Yuval-Davis, 1992). Similarly, White (often the unmarked norm) is in need of being deconstructed into its own internal differences. In both instances ethnicity offers categories for locating such differences. In Australia 'White' is an unmarked category implicitly opposed to Aborigines or Asians. But just as these categories in themselves need to be de-homogenised, so too 'White' needs to be unpacked, at the very least in order to dissociate older colonial settlers from those newer groups who settled in significant numbers after World War II. Here Australia's tradition of using multiculturalism as a way of distinguishing ethnic groups within Western and European frameworks offers a possible model for other societies to scrutinise. Australia, on the other hand, needs to rethink race in the light of analyses and distinctions that have taken place elsewhere in other comparable societies.

But let us pause here and rehearse some of the theoretical positions taken up around those poles of race and ethnicity—a particularly urgent task in the current climate of 'ethnic cleansing'.

The earliest use of the term 'ethnicity' had connotations of 'heathen' or 'pagan', but by about the nineteenth century the word had acquired implications of both 'race' and 'nation'. This reveals that ethnicity and race were linked from an early period. It also indicates certain assumptions about the nation and nationalism, namely that the secular is often linked to the theological, and that the secular narratives of nationalism often require a sacred justification (Anderson, 1991). In the seventeenth century, the adjacent term 'ethos' had the sense of a 'characteristic spirit, prevalent tone of sentiment of a people or community' (*OED*). This connotation underlies the current use of 'ethnicity' to distinguish between 'race' (in the biological sense) and 'custom' or 'history', or, to put it another way, between 'body' and 'spirit'. But before we move on to consider race, we should note that a second meaning of 'ethos' links it to aesthetic criticism and rhetoric, and to the portrayal of 'character through mimicry' (*OED*). Here, then, we have a highly charged chain of meanings with contemporary significance. As with the now outmoded distinction between 'sex' and socially constituted 'gender', one emphasises biological fact and the other a social construct . Nowadays, in the wake of the work of feminists such as Elizabeth Grosz (1994) and Moira Gatens (1990), we know that 'sexuality' is as much a construct as 'gender', and indeed that the body is as much an inscribed terrain as any other signifying system. Similarly, the old distinction between body and spirit no longer holds.

In the past, 'race' was invoked in comparable ways as a science for differentiating in essential (and thus essentialist) ways between the various peoples comprising humankind. Indeed, as the work of Donna Haraway (1989) shows, it was a way of distinguishing rather anxiously between humans and non-humans such as primates. As one of the 'irreducible' differences, 'race' conveyed a certain reassurance, as all such allegedly irrefutable distinctions do. 'Male' and 'female' are similar categories, each of which, as we know, has been confounded. 'Ethnicity', in contradistinction to 'race', was seen as a 'function of sociology and culture rather than biology' (Outlaw, 1990:60). For a while 'ethnicity' was the favoured term, because it was perceived as denoting a temporary state that would end eventually and inexorably in integration or assimilation. It was seen also in terms of individualism rather than relationship to a group, and the individual is never as threatening or potentially disruptive to the status quo as is the group. 'Ethnicity' had the quality of the self-chosen appellation; ethnic communities and ethnic identity are often perceived as being self-identified (Pearson, 1991); this remains a customary way of distinguishing 'ethnicity' from 'race'.

In Australian debates around ethnicity, 'race' dropped from usage as a classificatory term. It was replaced by 'ethnicity', which neither carried the same connotations of biological or physical reductionism nor had the same negative historical legacy (Kee, 1986), until the outbreak of civil war in the former Yugoslavia. Kee distinguishes 'ethnicity' from 'nationality', which indicates citizenship or legal status, and denotes adherence to the political unity of the nation-state. In other words, since we retain our nationality over and above our ethnic affiliations, 'nationality' allays the old fear that if the 'ethnics' were permitted to retain their *cultural* differences, they could not be trusted to maintain their *political* allegiance to Australia in times of crisis. Kee defines 'ethnicity' as a complex amalgam of language, religion, customs, symbols, literature, music, food and, at its core, an internal and external perception of difference. In other words, 'ethnicity' is defined by one's sense of both belonging to a group and being 'exclu[ded] from the national definition of a country' (Kee, 1986:7). Thus ethnicity appears to exist always in a marginal, and often negative, relationship to the mainstream or hegemonic group.

According to the 'poetics' of ethnicity developed by the US anthropologist Michael Fischer (1986), ethnicity is something reinvented for each generation; it represents a type of psychic excess that is not necessarily part of the conscious cognitive processes. Fischer locates it in the psychoanalytic terrain of dreaming and transference. It is predicated not on coherence but on the plural and the fragmentary, and takes for granted the several, often contradictory components, that comprise identity for the material subject caught up in a specific history. Thus ethnicity searches continuously for voices and not for a definitive stance. It seeks mutual illuminations in reading those juxtaposed dialogic texts or utterances that swerve away from the binary structures which traditionally have been the model for establishing the ground of culture. Perhaps most importantly of all, this particular way of conceiving of culture substitutes irony, one of the most intractable areas of so-called marginal or minority discourse, for authenticity. Irony is one of the most problematic characteristics for the mainstream to bestow on the marginal; it is apparently reserved for and is thus a mark of a dominant or privileged group. At its best, Fischer contends persuasively, ethnicity promotes the play between cultures, and emphasises that 'revelation of cultural artifice' which by its very nature deconstructs claims for cultural hegemony.

Like Fischer, Werner Sollors (1986:9) is also concerned with the invention of 'ethnicity', its codes, mental formations and cultural constructions. Sollors (ibid.:11) traces the role ethnicity has played in the movement in the US from a culture predicated on descent to one of consent: in other words, from notions of national cohesion (based on kinship or descent) to their necessary refor-mulation in a new world context of consent. In some ways ethnicity was a reminder of the old within the new, at least in the older scholarship on ethnic literatures. In contrast to this tradition, Sollors (ibid.:7) argues that ethnic literatures in fact provide grammars of new-world imagery and conduct. He also suggests that studies of ethnicity tend to homogenise ethnic groups and contrast them with those so-called 'unethnic' groups which con-stitute the unmarked majority (ibid.:178ff.). Even transnational cosmopolitanism, he suggests, is predicated on 'monistic little nationalities' (ibid.:185). He further makes the point that while ethnic literatures are in fact intertwined with the formal innova-tions associated with modernity, they tend to be seen in terms of content and unreconstructed parochialism rather than form (ibid.:237ff.; 1989:xix). Thus, repeatedly, we encounter in critical analyses of this writing a search for the traditional and the authen-tic. When writers from ethnic backgrounds become famous they are no longer marked as ethnic, since this equates them with the limited and the parochial (Sollors, 1986:41). Finally, he suggests that since ethnic writers always address at least a double audience, their work accommodates the play of particular kinds of irony (see also Hutcheon, 1991:69–95).

But how does ethnicity relate to race? Because references to 'race' fell into disrepute, especially after World War II, it seemed almost an insult to use the term. Increasingly it became clear that whereas there is no question of the reality of *racism*, the notion of 'racial purity' in biological or genetic terms, which underpins the concept of race, is a myth. At best one could talk only of 'clines', that is, 'gradients of change in terms of measurable genetic character such as skin colour' (Outlaw, 1990:64). At this juncture we might recall that the link between genes and culture is always problematic, and shapes such questions as, does one write differ-ently as a woman or as an 'ethnic'? Nowadays 'race' tends to be spoken of as a social formation rather than in terms of bloodlines. Indeed, to quote a current theorist on the subject, it is 'an unstable and decentred complex of social meanings constantly being trans-formed by political struggle . . . [and] political contestations over racial meanings' (ibid.:77).

But why are unproblematised references to race coming back

into circulation and not always negatively? For instance, 'Black' is a shifting term: in Australia, both Southern Europeans and Arabs refer to themselves as Black. Those involved in the Black struggle use the concept of race as a way of signalling their determination to resist assimilation and to pursue cultural difference and autonomy. In the Australian context, notes Fazal Rizvi in a forthcoming book, certain European (and other) groups such as Greeks and Italians, have been 'racialised' in very particular ways. The indigenous peoples of many cultures use the term 'race' because their culture has been disenfranchised and rendered invisible. And it is for similar reasons that other 'minority' groups also reach for the term. It embodies the magic of irreducible difference, a non-negotiable space which heralds a separate history, no less phantasmatic at its edges, however, than all histories. It is also tied in disturbing ways to the notion of primordial rights to land (Geertz, 1973)—disturbing because such claims about bloodlines and land have fuelled the fascist doctrines of recent history, including the upheavals in what used to be Yugoslavia.

In an important recent publication Floya Anthias and Nira Yuval-Davis (1992) analyse the various components that comprise the relationship between race and ethnicity. They conclude that no unitary system can be labelled racist, and that in fact it is not possible to distinguish in abstract terms between racial, ethnic and national collectivities. The only way of highlighting their differences is via their different histories, discourses and projects (ibid.:2–3). Focusing on ethnicity, they contend that discourses and practices around race have indeed become ethnicised. The racism directed at 'Blacks'—in England this tends to mean those whose countries of origin used to be part of the British empire (ibid.:147)—is embedded in the process of 'inferiorising' ethnic groups rather than being based on such biological differences as skin colour. Thus, to take other examples, Muslims are seen as 'non-civilised', and American Blacks are discriminated against because of the history of slavery rather than their skin colour (ibid.:133–7). Somewhat ominously, Anthias and Yuval-Davis contend that notions of cultural difference have displaced notions of biological difference as a basis for excluding or denigrating a group.

Like other theorists, they locate the basis of ethnicity in notions of community. In other words, there is too great a readiness to homogenise the ethnic community and to see continuities between ethnic groups and cultural groups. Culture in turn often collapses into religion, and when it does so it releases and gives legitimacy to varieties of fundamentalism (ibid.:193). If 'ethnicity' is simply located in unproblematic concepts of community, it becomes as generalised a category as 'race' tends to be, and does not allow for nuanced analyses. Nor should concepts of multiculturalism be reduced merely to the 'compatible boundaries of difference' (ibid.:196). In other words they must allow for both the incompatible and the incommensurable. This is a disturbing prospect for those who manage cultures in the name of cultural diversity.

Thus in many and various ways the idea of a homogeneous culture imbued with universal values has been undermined by those many perspectives which, in the past, were marginalised and excluded from the frame of reference which sustained such a concept. The next chapter will scrutinise more closely the ways in which a traditional minority framework, namely feminism, may in turn be challenged about its own exclusions when questions of cultural difference are posed in relation to the framing orthodoxies of sexual difference.

3

The Question of Authenticity: Feminist Theory and Minority Writing

> My sealed tomb
> Travels in my dreams. (Kefala, 1992:95)

Feminist theory has traditionally been an area where critics have searched for a framework for analysing the marginal. This is in part because the critical reception of both women's writing and ethnic minority writing has been haunted by questions of legitimation, founded on an authenticity supposedly based in experience. In other words, minority writing is characterised by offering the authority and authenticity of the marginal experience. Readers find that minorities are 'just like us', or so different that they throw the reader's own coherence into relief. That is to say, readers always rediscover themselves. Such are the problems of universalist readings, as distinct from attempts to develop strategies that enable us to read for difference. After Derrida, how might one argue for writing in conjunction with any notion of authenticity? Traditionally, authenticity has been located in speech and in the self which purports to be fully present behind the utterance. Writing, in Derrida's scheme, signals an orphaned textuality and a free play of meaning which go beyond the individual writer, whereas authenticity is associated with speech and voice, and functions precisely to reinforce 'the' individual as presence (Norris,1982:24–32). At the heart of postmodernist feminism is a paradox, succinctly expressed by Alice Jardine (1985:147): 'Feminism, while infinite in its variations, is finally rooted in the belief that women's truth-in-experience-and-reality is and has always been different from men's'.

This paradox continues to surface in various guises in many of the debates around feminist theory. It can be posed in other terms. Why should we read anyone in particular? Why should we insist on the rights of particular individuals to construct their own stories? How, indeed, might anyone be said to 'own' a story, if in writing we are dealing with a free play of signification? And what do we hope to see/hear when our ways of thinking about ourselves as fixed entities have been profoundly unsettled? How, in the wake of postmodernism, is it possible to theorise or clear a necessary space for the writings of particular subjects—for those who derive part of their subjectivity from minority groups, for example, or for those who are disadvantaged by signifying practices which privilege a majority as arbiters of what circulates as public meaning? As Catherine Belsey reminds us in her study of the subject:

> Subjectivity is discursively produced and is constrained by the range of subject-positions defined by the discourses in which the concrete individual participates . . . In this sense existing discourses determine not only what can be said and understood, but the nature of subjectivity itself, what it is possible to be . . . Since meaning is plural, to be able to speak is to be able to take part in the contest for meaning which issues in the production of new subject-positions, new determinations of what it is possible to be. (Belsey, 1985:5–6)

But how might one argue for those 'new determinations' and resistances as coming from and privileging a particular group, without returning or reconsolidating that humanist subjectivity which traditionally is constituted as male, bourgeois, European and universal (speaking for all)? Some years ago, efforts to clear a space for women's writing generated a great deal of debate over whether or not one could claim the authority to write on the basis of a difference which apparently had not yet been represented. As Anne Freadman (1985:168) argued, 'theories of representation . . . assume the world itself to be the arbiter of accuracy'; and, indeed, women's writing claimed its legitimation on the grounds of a prior world, namely women's own experiential truths. This controversy over whether or not women write differently—simply by being that unproblematic category 'woman'—still surfaces (see the critique by Moi, 1985, particularly Part 1). It became increasingly clear that this strategy burdened women once again with biological essentialism, and thus imprisoned them in a determinism which precluded social change. Such arguments reinforced that concept of a passive and unreflective 'feminine' which in the writings of men has always been the inferior component in a binary category. This was arguably so even when it took the extremely subtle form of *écriture féminine*, as Toril Moi (1985:121–6) has argued concerning the work of Hélène Cixous. Women do not write differently by virtue of being born with wombs but because they learn to become women. This counter-thesis is rooted in Simone de Beauvoir's famous and elegantly concise dictum that women are made and not born. Later versions have gained strength from Christine Delphy's (1984) argument for a redefinition of knowledge which takes into account the materialism of women's lives and historical oppression. They have benefited also from Teresa de Lauretis's redefinition of the category of experience itself, even though she has been criticised for underestimating the importance of the unconscious in this process:

I use the term not in the individualistic, idiosyncratic sense of something belonging to one and exclusively her own even though others might have 'similar' experiences; but rather in the general sense of a process by which, for all social beings, subjectivity is constructed. Through that process one places oneself or is placed in social reality, and so perceives and comprehends as subjective (referring to, even originating in, oneself) those relations—material, economic, and interpersonal—which are in fact social and, in a larger perspective, historical. The process is continuous, its achievement unending or daily renewed. For each person, therefore, subjectivity is an ongoing construction, not a fixed point of departure or arrival from which one then interacts with the world. On the contrary, it is the effect of that interaction—which I call experience; and thus it is produced not by external ideas, values, or material causes, but by one's personal, subjective, engagement in the practices, discourses, and institutions that lend significance (value, meaning, and affect) to the events of the world. (de Lauretis, 1984:159)

Such critiques focus increasingly on materialism (in the sense of the continuous construction and reconstruction of subjectivity) rather than biologism. In other words, women write and read differently in so far as they live out their lives as socially categorised women and in so far as their texts circulate or are consumed differently from those stamped with male signatures. Even those women whose writings/readings are superficially indistinguishable from those of men none the less negotiate a different kind of access to signifying practices and to discursive formations. They may be perceived as practising a type of mimicry which, even when self-consciously executed, is arguably limited in its subversive effects (Moi, 1985:140–3). There is also Joan Scott's illuminating analysis of 'what counts as experience'. 'Subjects are constituted discursively', she contends, ' and experience is a linguistic event (it doesn't happen outside established meanings), but neither is it confined to a fixed order of meaning . . . What counts as experience is neither self-evident nor straightforward; it is always contested, and always therefore political' (Scott, 1991: 793–7). Current projects concerned with redefining the interactions between the somatic and psychic body promise to develop new theoretical arguments in support of the specificities of women's writing, while assiduously avoiding any biological essentialism (Schor,1985; Grosz, 1994).

These developments in feminist materialisms are important in the face of a feminist orthodoxy which might be described as the emergence of a unified female subjectivity, which is the flip side of the humanist (male) subjectivity referred to earlier. In response to postmodernism, and in the face of increasing critiques from so-called marginal women's groups, the 'feminist subject' has been seen to be just as ethnocentric and exclusive, just as imperialist and bourgeois, as her male counterpart in claiming to speak on behalf of all women.[1]

As a result of such critiques—and a recognition that the oppositional model will always see-saw between contending unified subjectivities—it has become more expedient than ever to shift the emphasis to a decentred subject or subjects-in-process in order to open up different kinds of discursive resistances, which result, as Belsey argues, in different possibilities for social meanings. It helps to remember also that Lyotard's (1984) oft-quoted definition of postmodernism associates an 'incredulity toward meta-narratives' with a concomitant movement toward 'local determinism'.[2] These local determinisms have kinship with Belsey's discursive resistances. That postmodernism represents a total break with modernism is not being argued here at all; indeed, Lyotard (1986) has repeatedly defined the much-maligned 'post' as a return (as in anamnesis) to what has been forgotten, rather than as a leaving behind. The emphasis here is on minor and heterogeneous narratives which come from outside the known canons and literary traditions. In the last decade feminist scholars have recovered many lost female writers, and this has resulted in the formation of a female great tradition which does of course represent certain pleasures and satisfactions, particularly for women.

But, simultaneously, one becomes conscious of exclusions. This is symptomatic, of course, of any canon formation. Even when those exclusions are noted—and there is a scramble to read, for example, varieties of non-European women writers—the *way* in which they are read derives often from familiar and Eurocentric perspectives. At the same time the marketplace is attempting to capture ever more exotic 'outsiders' and recruit them to publishers' lists. The effect has been ambiguous. On the one hand there has been a welcome diversification of Eurocentric and bourgeois literary canons; on the other such writings have also served to consolidate the genre of the first-person confessional novel (the promulgation of the truth-speaking subject) to which all women's writing was assigned initially. Woman as Truth has returned in the guise of working-class, Black, lesbian and other varieties of minority women, and has been constructed as much in opposition to hegemonic women as to hegemonic men.

The delineations of oppression and silencing manifest in these texts served to reinforce, renew and legitimate those original claims for promoting women's writing which were offered in the 1960s and 1970s. The more women's writing there was, the less plausible became women's claims that they were silenced or textually absent. Consequently, new witnesses to oppression were required. Not that the struggle to introduce women's texts into teaching institutions is by any means over, for tales of continuing battles prevail. But there is no doubt that women's writing has enjoyed a spectacular marketing success. As ever, feminists are alert to the spectre of 'recuperation', which is the name given to modes of reading which co-opt a radical text for a conservative or even reactionary agenda. The emphasis should now be on rereading these newly conscripted texts and being alert to their differences, instead of treating them as a chorus of women's voices blended in undifferentiated sisterhood. That impulse to homogenise is a feminist version of imperialism.

Increasingly, and not just within feminism, so-called minority writings are privileged as part of a general strategy for dismantling the humanist subject. Julia Kristeva (1980, 1982), for example, recruits dissident male avant-garde texts to the domain of the subversive semiotic, which exists prior to the symbolic and continues to disrupt it. On the other hand, there is Deleuze and Guattari's distinction between majority and minority literatures:

> In major literatures . . . the individual concern (familial, marital, and so on) joins with other no less individual concerns, the social milieu serving as a mere environment or a background . . . The three characteristics of minor literature are the deterritorialization of language, the connection of the individual to political immediacy, and the collective assemblage of enunciation. We might say that minor no longer designates specific literatures but the revolutionary conditions for every literature within the heart of what is called great (or established) literature. (Deleuze and Guattari, 1986:17–18)

In the case of those newly discovered exclusions from the female canon described above, the forms have *not* been shattered. Rather, the emphasis has been on 'speaking' (a manifestation of female presence) and content; in other words, such texts have been read as reinforcing a major and established literature, and not for their differences. If, for the moment, we accept Deleuze and Guattari's (ibid.:19) distinction, it comes down to being a stranger in one's own language and rereading it from the outside. Here an understanding of 'minority' is central as a method for breaking through privileged meanings. When does one start/stop being part of a minority? One is not necessarily born into a minority. Instead, it is a question of being alert to the positionings involved, particularly one's own as reader. We return necessarily to the issue of 'experience' and how it serves materialism, the daily construction of subjectivity. And we return also to Jardine's statement that 'feminism, while infinite in its variations, is finally rooted in the belief that women's truth-in-experience-and-reality is and has always been different from men's' (Jardine, 1985:147).

If we subscribe to the project of deconstructing those binary oppositions which continue to trap 'women' in the service of that origin of meaning and truth, the male humanist subject, then how can we at the same time endorse feminist enterprises which assert truths located in women's empirical experience, especially when we have been at such pains to tease out the ways in which 'experience' has always consolidated the imaginary relations of ideology? 'The politics of experience', according to Jane Gallop, 'is inevitably a conservative politics for it cannot help but conserve traditional ideological constructs which are not recognised as such but are taken for the "real"' (quoted in ibid.:155). If we recognise the politics of Gallop's dictum, then on what theoretical grounds is it possible to argue that women should write and read as women, much less that particular groups of women should write and read on their own political behalf? If we are in the process of questioning such things as truth-claims (which comprise, among other things, Lyotard's master-narratives of Western philosophy and Derrida's metaphysics of presence, phonocentrism and the privileging of voice) how then might we respond to any minority's struggle to speak and to write? That question necessarily focuses on the struggle to read in new ways without reconstructing the old hierarchies and oppositions of signification.

Take the example of ethnic minority women's writing in Australia. In analysing the way in which ethnic minority writing is positioned within Australian writing, Althusser's concept of 'interpellation' remains useful: it refers to that 'hailing into being' of the subject which is constitutive of ideology (Althusser, 1976; for a critique see Hirst, 1979). Althusser defines ideology as the subject's imaginary relations to real social conditions. The concept of interpellation is useful in spite of the fact that it is arguably based on the notion of a unified and conscious subject. For the subject could not acknowledge this institutional 'hailing into being' unless some kind of subjectivity existed prior to interpellation. Attention has also been drawn to this hailing as a 'misrecognition' related in some ways to that misrecognition described in Lacanian accounts of the mirror stage of psychic development (Burniston and Weedon, 1978). In other ways it is quite different, of course, because the Althusserian interpellated subject does not have an unconscious. In relation to ethnic minority writing, interpellation focuses on the institutional processes which assign human subjects to particular positions, and on the inevitable misrecognitions which result. It is not that ethnic minorities are invisible in Australian discursive formations, but that they are positioned only in certain areas: sociology, oral history, welfare legislation, etc. They are consistently 'hailed into being' as speaking subjects but not as writing subjects. To put it another way, the possibility that other subjectivities exist—for example, in former cultures or languages— is precisely *not* interpellated in the Australian context except in negative or crude ways. That they are therefore fragmented or decentred subjects is perhaps more overt than is the case with other groups. But they are not read in this way. Instead, ethnic minority women are interpellated in Anglo-Celtic Australian culture as signifying sexuality (they breed), food (they over-feed their families), factory fodder (they supplement family incomes by part-time and below-award work), and silence (they never learn English because they don't mix with the wider community and so are, effectively, silent).

This may be illustrated further in a film produced by the Department of Immigration in the 1950s called *No Strangers Here*, where there is a brilliant *mise en abyme* or miniaturisation of the problem.[3] The film is set in 'Littletown', a small Australian rural town, in the immediate postwar period. Narrative point of view is provided by the editor of the town's newspaper, a genial and overweight liberal. The story begins when he receives several anonymous letters, signed 'a true Australian', basically saying that foreigners are not wanted in Littletown. As the editor perambulates through the town kissing babies and talking to women, he notices the arrival of a foreign and good-looking nuclear family. A voice-over traces their backgrounds briefly as refugees from totalitarian and war-torn Europe. Their exact provenance is carefully not specified. Suffice to say that they clearly gesture their astonishment at the abundance of material objects around them: food and particularly a bicycle, which the father craves. Remarkably quickly they find their niches. The father works in the brickworks, the son goes to school, and the fetching daughter ends up as an aide in the local hospital, where she sets the hearts of the male patients and doctors aflutter. The mother remains in the home, where the editor decides to pay her a visit. He enters her home with the immortal words: 'Please tell me the story of your life!' On the brink of answering, the mother rushes to the oven, where something more urgent is evidently calling for attention. She offers the editor a slice of home-made cake and he in turn requests the recipe. This proves to be the answer to his question. The recipe is published under the heading 'Easy To Mix' and the town's women respond appropriately.

This risible small tale is actually an extremely accurate metaphoric and metonymic delineation of the ideology at the heart of postwar migration and the various attempts to manage it. The film signals assimilation in certain ways, notably linking it to the digestive model from which the term derives. Crucially, the mother offers food instead of words. Food, as we know, has long been the acceptable face of multiculturalism.

One way of exploring this signifying chain is Julia Kristeva's linking of the concept of 'abjection' to language, food and the mother. Subject-formation in *No Strangers Here* is constituted in terms of language and food. In Australia, one of the few non-threatening ways to speak of multiculturalism is in relation to food; all these ethnic minorities, it is said, have improved the diversity of the national cuisine. The usual and acceptable way of celebrating this diversity is through a multicultural food festival.

Julia Kristeva (1982:4) defines the 'abject' as an ambiguous area surrounding borderlines. It threatens the stability of subject-formation through problems engendered by separation from the mother. It is a place where meanings are lost, 'the in-between, the ambiguous, the composite'. Her introductory example relates to food, namely, the inexplicable revulsion experienced at the prospect of ingesting the skin which forms on milk. As her study goes on to reveal, the abject is related to the mother in the most primal sense, as that from which the subject needs to become detached in order to form a separate ego. The mother links not only food, meaning and language, but also entry into the symbolic, the law which gives meaning to social negotiations. The mother is subsequently relegated to the semiotic hinterland where monsters dwell. Interestingly, in Kristeva's analysis, the phobic who endures the abject often displays remarkable linguistic versatility. Hence the reference to Little Hans (ibid.:34) and his obsessive need to name everything as a way of warding off his fear of the unnamable:

> . . . the phobic object is a proto-writing and, conversely, any practice of speech, inasmuch as it involves writing, is a language of fear. . . the writer is a phobic who succeeds in metaphorizing in order to keep from being frightened of death; instead he comes to life in signs. (ibid.:38)

To some extent this relates also to Freud's notion of the uncanny, although Kristeva differentiates it from this by pointing out that there is nothing familiar in the abject, 'not even the shadow of a memory' (ibid.:5). In her study of the monstrous female, Barbara Creed (1986) relates the abject to the mother who must be expelled lest she devour her offspring—the all-engulfing image. Again, the mother, food, and the loss of meaning are clearly linked. The suggestion here is that foreign languages function in a predominantly Anglophone context as the abject, as something which threatens meaning and subject-formation, including the notion of a coherent national identity. Words are feared because, unlike food, they cannot be assimilated, and words in another language emphasise the split within subjectivity. Words are able, like the non-introjected mother, to devour from within.

To consider ethnic minority women's writing in Australia, one is forced to add to the complications of gendered readings both culture (particularly in its foreignness or incommensurability, as analysed above) and, to some extent, class. In the early days the field of women's writing was always dominated by first-person confessional or semi-autobiographical writings. The mode was realist, and there seemed to be little problematising of the first person singular; consequently, one appeared when reading such writing to be encountering unified subjects who offer revelations about gender. In the name of that 'I', and in order to develop certain political agendas such as adding women to teaching institutions and to canons, questions of writing (in the Derridean sense) seemed a luxury women could not afford. Here then was a female metaphysics of presence, and here were new 'master'-narratives. Comparably, in ethnic minority writing, a harvest of first-person accounts has been used to fuel a tradition of oral history which began with efforts to insert class differences into the narratives of Australian history. Like the working-class, ethnic minorities were another disadvantaged group testifying to the democratisation of the history machine in Australia. Ethnic minority 'speech', rather than writing, served the larger projects of 'assimilation' and 'naturalisation', the latter being a term that very aptly labels those strategies which consolidate the bourgeois, male, European humanist subject as beyond question the natural, invisible and omnipotent embodiment of commonsense. Thus ethnic minorities and women were constructed not as subjects-in-process (in the sense derived from Kristeva,1980:124–47), but as apprentice subjects on the way to achieving unified subjectivity in the discursive formations of history and sociology. There women's problems became 'women as problem', and problems experienced by ethnic minorities similarly became 'the ethnic minority as problem' (Henriques, 1984:60–89). This schema represents a remedial approach to the question of culture or gender inequality that is reflected in the ways in which those writings are received: at best they are read as naive, and at worst as linguistically incompetent.[4]

To stress different ways of reading is not to suggest that these texts should be read simply in terms of female otherness because, as has often been pointed out, the other is often designated as female (Jardine, 1985:31; Lloyd,1984), and the effect of such enterprises is to confirm and legitimate what is already known and said. It is more appropriate, therefore, to remember that a concept often excludes the conditions of its existence (Lyotard,1984:81). But how do we begin to think of such writings as not coming from everywhere but as having the history and positionality of writings from somewhere?

The hypothesis advanced here is that 'ethnic minority women's writing' signals more clearly than other kinds the ideological loadings of its 'hailing into being', precisely because it registers that interpellation as involving a split. Ethnic minority writing carries within it (to put it another way) the dead or repressed or fading subjects created by other and former interpellations. Hence the quotation as opening epigraph from Antigone Kefala's poem 'Inheritance':

> My sealed tomb
> Travels in my dreams.

Some of this writing breaks down any obvious reading of a subjectivity unified according to gender, class and culture, because it registers clearly its dissonance from the traditional processes of meaning. This is not true of all such writing, however, because some of it also plays the games of mimicry, 'passing', and creating familiar facsimiles of the subjects we all know. In the writings considered in this study—the work of Ania Walwicz, Antigone Kefala, Rosa Cappiello and Anna Couani—the use of the first person singular is overtly problematic. Nobody, of course, is ever fully interpellated as a subject, for there is *always* a misrecognition. But those who are interpellated in ways which so totally fall short of other reflections—that is, when the gap between imaginary relations and real conditions becomes an abyss—reach as a matter of survival for the first-person pronoun in order to establish some kind of foothold. It is precisely here, under those conditions, that 'truth' (in the sense of a reality beyond our experience) is signalled as contingent, as historically and culturally specific. And it is here also that subjectivity is fragmented into contradictory positions which are also historically and culturally specific.

In answer to her own formulation of the paradox being addressed, Alice Jardine locates the following answer:

> I discovered that the differences between the male-written and female-written texts of modernity were not, after all, in their so-called 'content', but in their enunciation: in their modes of discourse ('sentimental', ironic, scientific, etc.); in their twisting of female obligatory connotations, of inherited genealogies of the feminine; in their haste or refusal to use the pronouns 'I' or 'we'; in their degree of willingness to gender those pronouns as female; in their adherence to or dissidence from feminism as a movement; in the tension between their desire to remain radical and their desire to be taken seriously as theorists and writers in what remains a male intellectual community; in the extent of their desire to prescribe what posture women should adopt toward the new configurations of woman in modernity; in the intensity of their desire to privilege women as proto-modernists. (Jardine, 1985:260–1)

The claims about proto-modernism are not unrelated to those advanced here on behalf of ethnic minority women's writing, although the emphases differ. In both cases, it is a question of when a subject-in-process speaks (history), how (enunciation), and from where (positionality). Such texts provoke in Australian reviewers what might be termed aggressive nostalgia. Australian culture is being transformed rapidly into nostalgic texts that solidify the last two hundred years into the 'way we were' in the course of consolidating the new republicanism. After all, Australian literature has been constructed into a literary tradition only recently. To question its national comprehensiveness at this stage (when Australian cultural pundits are busily enshrining nationalism in conjunction with identity) will of course provoke hostility.[5] While such texts provoke a nostalgia which sends many Australian readers scurrying back to Anglo-Celtic cultural solidarity, they also carry their own kinds of nostalgia for Old Greece or Old Italy. As Cappiello's narrator remarks sardonically, 'Everyone's got a right to a glorious past' (Cappiello, 1984:55).

What Walwicz, Kefala, Cappiello and Couani have in common is their representation of consciousness by montage, a technique which is non-realist and resists narrative closure. 'There is only collage, cutting and splicing', writes Virilio. 'We're in the age of micro-narratives, the art of the fragment' (Virilio and Lotringer, 1983:35). These are the short narratives and atomisations to which Lyotard (1984:14–17) refers within the context of postmodernism. They also offer parodic readings of culture and gender, both in relation to 'Australia' and to 'Europe'. The question is always, for whom? We need of course to ask how these texts differ from other kinds of non-realist or experimental writing in Australia. They differ only in so far as they foreground specific historical and cultural socio-political questions about pronouns and positionality: who, from where, when and to whom? They remind those who have eyes to see that the enunciating positions are partial and outside, or overlapping with manifestations of other cultural codes. The first-person pronoun, when used, is more often than not parodic of the first-person confessional, as in Walwicz's two poems 'Photos' (Walwicz, 1982a: xx) and 'I' (in Gunew, 1987a: 134). Elsewhere, it is rendered as uncanny:

> I have set my life aside
> placed it in the shade
> of the familiar room
> where it waits speechless.
> My other self moves now,
> Laughs in the morning light,
> watches the twilight, indigo,
> remote, ungrasped,
> the faint memory of a sensation
> that has stirred in me sometimes,
> gone now,
> vanishing with the evening. (Kefala, 1992:98)

Perhaps it is appropriate to emphasise here that ethnic minority writing is authenticated not simply by entering Australia with a foreign passport and a first language other than English. But if we agree with Teresa de Lauretis that experience includes the continuous construction of subjectivity (including processes of signification), then these texts clearly manifest a cultural and linguistic dislocation across .gender, class, and so on, which averts easy closures.

Ethnic minority women's writings 'denaturalise' readings of them by outsiders,[6] including feminists. They remind us that the subject-in-process—as derived from psychoanalytic and post-structuralist theory—has a specific historical context. In their use of irony and their appeal to double audiences, such texts undo the legitimations usually conferred on minority writing. The following chapters explore some of these claims further in relation to specific writers and texts.

Reading for Cultural Difference

4

In Journeys Begin Dreams: Antigone Kefala and Ania Walwicz

In dreams begins the journey . . . (Kefala, 1973:5)

How easy is it, even now, to attach notions of the literary to ethnic minority writing? If not, then what are the implications for practitioners who wish to participate in selecting the words which, according to Barthes, consolidate social meaning? 'Literature remains the currency in use in a society apprised, by the very form of words, of the meaning of what it consumes' (Barthes, 1967:38). What kind of signification is ethnic minority writing permitted within Australia? Such writing is not usually received as 'literature' which, for the moment, can be described as a textuality which is visibly more worked over, and more conscious of textual conventions, than other forms of writing, and whose implicit opposite is the apparent 'disorder' of speech (ibid.:25). If we accept the suggestion that ethnic minority writing signifies only within the formations of sociology and history then, paradoxically, its value lies here with speech rather than writing. In other words, when made synonymous with migrant writing, it is the migrant's speech (rather than writing) which is solicited, and the more disordered it is the more authentic it supposedly sounds. In those terms, ethnic minority writing is valued precisely in so far as it is inscribed with the marks of linguistic naivety and (even) incompetence: broken language is perceived as symptomatic of subjects not yet 'assimilated' (rendered the same) or 'naturalised'.

In the little writing of this kind which receives limited exposure (whether autobiographical or autobiographically based), any obvious signs that the language has been crafted are read none the less as relatively unmediated confessions (see Chapter 5). Complexities, if acknowledged, are thought of as provided by 'life', the complicated history of the migrant or marginalised subject—rather than by any consciously wrought textuality. To consider ethnic minority poetry, for instance, is under those circumstances therefore perverse. Poetry, the least transparently functional manifestation of linguistic self-consciousness, can be read only with difficulty for sociological or historical content. In Barthes' terms, classical poetry is 'a speech which is made more socially acceptable by virtue of the very conspicuousness of its conventions' (ibid.:48). To write poetry means that one is staking a claim to the literary and hence to public cultural participation. On what grounds can this be legitimated, more particularly when the language used is patently either not English, or, if English, then filtered through other languages and literary traditions with their own codes, canons and conventions? Those 'conspicuous conventions' alluded to by Barthes are not simply acquired when setting foot on this continent, nor are they part of the naturalisation certificate. Rather, they belong to that cultural ghosting which floats above the home territory and signifies a mystery only gradually comprehended after many rites of passage. Poetry? From ethnic minorities? Classic realist narratives, perhaps, and reluctantly, but not poetry.

To some extent, as I have argued elsewhere (Gunew, 1985), the experience of migration, particularly when it involves negotiating another language, changes the conditions governing signification. In some ways, speaking psychoanalytically, it may be seen as analogous to re-entering the Lacanian symbolic (Wilden, 1968:xii), or (in classic Freudian terms) changing the secondary, censoring processes of the preconscious (Silverman, 1983). In either model we are dealing with a foundational process in the construction of human subjectivity, namely the conditions under which subjects both participate in and are produced by signification. To enter language is to become a social being rescued from the incoherence and anarchy of drives, 'the mental representative of a somatic impulse' (ibid.:67); but inevitably this is achieved at the cost of certain repressions, including degrees of alienation from the drive.[1]

In the last few decades there have been considerable efforts to mark the discursive formation of Australian literature, in gendered and cultural terms, as predominantly Anglo-Celtic and male. Hence the work of those who consider the implications of treating Aboriginal writing as either true to oral traditions or colonised by white forms (Davis and Hodge, 1985; Benterrak, Muecke and Roe, 1984), and also of those who see women's writing as throwing new light on, for example, foundation myths of mateship and the bush (Modjeska, 1981; Ferrier, 1985; Schaffer, 1988). The further complications offered by poetry written from non-Anglo-Celtic perspectives raise questions about the modernity of such writings that relate as much to form as content (Sollors, 1986). Those able to think from the beginning in more than one language find it impossible to consider language as a 'natural' and unproblematic expression of experience. And those who have experience of more than one culture may find it more difficult to regard one culture as universal. As David Malouf points out:

> What we may have to be vigilant about is the groups in our society who feel that the culture belongs to them, who insist that their version of the culture is central or the only authentic one. Mostly the only cultural history we get of a society is the one that is passed down to us by those who have power, privilege and the use of language. (Malouf, 1985:61)

The reception of Walwicz and Kefala has been instructive in so far as it can be read symptomatically to gauge the ways in which ethnic minority writers are positioned in Australian culture. Let us consider Kefala first.

> I am tired, living at home among strangers,
> sitting at the same tables,
> waiting for an acceptance that never comes,
> an understanding that would not be born,
> the measure in us already spent. (Kefala, 1973:8)

It is arguably easier to forget a language than to banish the various selves forged by it, since it is through language that we are forced to contend with the nuances of gender, culture, race and class. And when that mirror is veiled or shattered? To change a language is to change one's selves; these are always plural and fragmented, just as dictionaries barely harness the anarchic excess of even one language between their rigid covers.The austerity of Kefala's writing (misread by some as a lack of attention to concrete detail) testifies constantly to these states of precarious subjectivity, lifted free of contextualising mutabilities. Kefala's refusal to 'tell stories' in any simple sense (as identified disparagingly by one early reviewer) is perhaps, more accurately, a refusal to abide by the conventions of classic narrative, with its emphasis on closure and sequential events. She seems concerned rather with being and becoming, the conscious and the unconscious, and hence with dreams and thoughts in preference to events: 'In dreams begins the journey' (ibid.:5).

The reception of her work over the years shows the difficulties Australian reviewers have in dealing with anything other than classic realist texts, and particularly if it comes from an ethnic minority writer. Hence the bewildered tone of those reviewers who accuse her of 'committing' novellas instead of 'proper' novels or, at the very least, seemly short stories. 'There are far too many seemingly gratuitous passages', wrote one such reviewer, 'such as long descriptions of characters who are peripheral or of scenes which are not integrated into the story' (Thorne, 1976). Kefala's earlier reviewers speak from the stability of a common language which assumes that English is never subject to the seismic disturbances of history, class, race or gender, and that Australian English, as developed over almost two hundred years, should not be fissured by the many dialects which produced those numerous groups of voyagers. From whence do these reviewers derive their authority to speak in the name of 'Australia' and of 'literature'? Presumably, as always, it amounts to a matter of access to the processes and institutions of literature.

Often it is not so much the writer's words which are being assimilated as her biographical exotica, including the strikingly iconic photographs which frame each of her books. Thus, unsurprisingly, early reviews refer to her 'femininity' and 'vulnerability' (Shapcott, 1973:135; Dutton, 1978:62) without needing to explain these terms. They would appear to be confirmed by the signifier of the poet's photograph, which in the second book of poems, ironically, presents her with her back turned upon a mirror. This does not prevent her from being received, however, in terms of that trope of the 'feminine': reflected surfaces (Kefala, 1978). This putative female terrain is predictably taken up by another reviewer as 'private' and 'constantly groping', driven by a supposed compulsion to write (Kim, 1976). How often women writers are described as being afflicted with these 'instinctive' pressures, and their works reduced to their 'femininity' and 'female corporeality' (see Ellmann, 1979, esp. ch. 3). And what are we to do with the following, which begs a number of questions?

> The cover picture of the author, the first-person form, and something about the style combine to imply a female protagonist. When the reader learns otherwise it is surprising but not jarring. The impressions maintain a non-masculine air but never shy from youthful male sexual awareness. The description of the people is subtly sexual but unbound by the usual confines of sexual perspective. (Stender, 1977:19)

The foreign name is also a signifier which appears to function independently of the texts produced 'in its name'. Critics apparently allow the authorial signature to pre-empt the space of the text. Assumptions made on the basis of the signature engender reviews which evoke heroic voices and references to 'the elegance of hundreds of years of mannered Europe' (Vaughan, 1979:24) or to 'Greek epics of passage as told by ancient voices' (Lindsay, 1979: 65). Another review refers to a 'tragic and uniquely Greek mood of un-belonging' more at home in 'the wintry Balkans' than 'the bright Aegean' (Junius, 1976). Such links between signature and presumed tradition continue to be made, as is illustrated in a more recent review of *European Notebook* (Kefala, 1988a), according to which 'many of Kefala's poems read as if they have been well-translated from a modern Greek poet under the influence of such masters as Seferis and Ritsos' (Page, 1979). I am reminded here of Peggy Kamuf's well-known study of the complications provided by the signature in a deconstructive frame:

> As a piece of proper name, the signature points, at one extremity, to a properly unnameable singularity; as a piece of language, the signature touches, at the other extremity, on the

space of free substitution without proper reference. At the edge of the work, the dividing trait of the signature pulls in both directions at once: appropriating the text under the sign of the name, expropriating the name in the play of the text. (Kamuf, 1988:12–13)

Other reviews complain about a 'lack of any structural development' (Kim, 1976) in *The First Journey* (Kefala, 1975), a book which blurs the boundary between poetry and prose but is not seen as good enough in its own right to merit a new term for its new form. Another reviewer praises the novella 'The Boarding House' (ibid.) because the writer is aided and abetted by readers already familiar with the Sydney setting (Thorne, 1976). A familiarity with whose Sydney is being invoked here? Finally, what are we to make of this? 'If there is a fault to be found, it is in too great a reliance upon set images (however appropriate they are) cast within one tone of voice and one philosophical framework, little advanced upon "The Alien"' (Lindsay, 1979:65). What can one do in the face of being 'condemned' for producing both a distinctive 'voice' and a coherent philosophy?

Antigone Kefala came to Australia via Romania, Greece and New Zealand, where she received her tertiary education (Kefala, 1988b). Her prose works clearly explore gender roles, especially *The First Journey* (Kefala, 1975) and *The Island* (Kefala, 1984a). Kefala's poetry, however, establishes a narrator who is not easily or consistently gendered, but who clearly derives from a 'foreign' culture, in so far as it evokes a contrapuntal cultural vision (Said, 1984b), both inside and outside the culture being observed. The informing perspective is positioned in a bourgeois European cultural tradition, from which the first two volumes of poetry comment on both New Zealand and Australia, as can be seen by looking at the juxtapositions of her collected work to date. The worlds created in *The First Journey, Alexia* (Kefala, 1984b), *European Notebook* (Kefala, 1988a) and *Absence* (Kefala, 1992) depict an intimately conjured-up world of European émigrés. Dreams play a significant role, but in very different ways from, say, the work of Ania Walwicz, which is discussed below.

When one is deprived of a collective unconscious, in the sense of a shared body of mythic underpinnings to experience, what is left but a recourse to personal dreams? Kefala inserts into her poems what often appear to be very personal and idiosyncratic dream sequences; but this characteristic may be, more precisely, a strategy for constituting a new body of myth. In other words, the ostensibly personal is in fact a way of moving beyond the specific individual to that territory of the personal which everyone shares. The Jungian concept of the collective unconscious is not quite appropriate here, for as Lacan would have it, the unconscious is always collective (that is, social) and functions moreover like a language, which is also social. It may therefore be more accurate to speak of a mythic dimension (including the ritualisation of daily acts) which comprises a crucial element in that elusive concept we term 'culture'. We all dream but not all cultures acknowledge the importance of circulating dreams as part of the daily, fully conscious life. If one is displaced to a part of the world where public dreaming (a mythic system) has quite different resonances, or none at all, what remains but to draw attention to this absence and to begin to fashion a new mythography?

> Dreaming allows for, supports, releases, brings to light an extreme delicacy of moral, sometimes even metaphysical, sentiments, the subtlest sense of human relations, refined differences, a learning of the highest civilization, in short a conscious logic, articulated with an extraordinary finesse, which only an intense waking labor would be able to achieve. In short, dreaming makes everything in me which is not strange, foreign, speak: the dream is an uncivil anecdote made up of very civilized sentiments (the dream is civilizing). (Barthes, 1975: 59–60)[2]

The first words of Kefala's earliest collection are, 'In dreams begins the journey' (Kefala, 1973:5). Australian and New Zealand culture and myth are predicated upon journeys, so that the chord touched here creates a group of readers who can indeed concur, at some level, that we (non-indigenous peoples) are all immigrants, particularly in the sense that the concerns of modernity are intimately bound up with migration and displacement (Carter, 1992; Papastergiadis, 1993). Immediately after this tenuously shared territory is established, there evolves a landscape utterly foreign to Anglo-Celtic readers:

> In dreams begins the journey, they would say
> moving the candle in the darkened room
> that smelt of cherry jam and basil.
> I watched their shadows moving on the walls
> straining to hear the corners creaking in the dark
> afraid of the black night that fell outside
> in silent, feathered sheets, of the abandoned
> courtyard, save for the big dogs,
> and far away the well. (Kefala, 1973:5)

In so far as the cherry jam, basil, courtyard and well constitute a familiar foreignness, it vaguely conjures up a (possibly) Greek territory already textualised by the nineteenth-century Romanticism of Byron or the twentieth-century romanticism of Lawrence Durrell. Those to whom it speaks with utter familiarity are Greek Australians (or Greek New Zealanders). The landscape evoked in the poem lacks distracting detail, as in old photos. The narrator recalls a childhood and a hidden menace of adult voices issuing from darkness with their prohibitions, hinting at the dead and the threats of the past. The escape, in the last stanza, attributed to the (possibly) dead 'Katka', evokes a childhood Land of Cockayne which dispels the dark: 'And you are the light, shadowless, falling/ upon these fields forever petrified in silence' (ibid.). These ambiguous last lines make it unclear whether it is the 'fields' or the 'you' which will be forever 'petrified in silence'. References to gender have intruded earlier, linking women, the well, the darkness, 'wild men's eyes' and again the notion of silence ('dumb mouths').

The gender of the narrator in 'Memory' (ibid.:17) is hinted at only through the introductory quotation from Sophocles' *Antigone*. Antigone—that proper name from Western myth, who puts family ties above duty to the state—figures, not unexpectedly, in this poet's private pantheon. Here again we are presented with the motif of being uprooted, this time in conjunction with the dutiful daughter who guards both father and brother. Antigone, daughter of Oedipus, shares his exile, and after his apotheosis defies her uncle in order to bury her rebel brother.

The opening lines of the poem address the epigraph and signal the context of exile, both from country and from sustaining Gods (significantly, these are plural and capitalised, for we are not on familiar Christian soil). The second stanza moves into a dream where a maternal 'I' cradles a 'you' suffering from 'some dark disease'—possibly the exile itself, or something more. Men in uniform converge silently. In the second part the 'you' remains fitfully lost in the darkness, but sometimes recaptures the 'far country' of the past with its 'stray sunray, some meaning'. The 'you' is distinguished from an 'us' who are protected by 'narrow knowledge . . . and our social ways'. The third section evokes a 'common house' of locked doors and men in white:

'They steal my time', you said in a low voice.
Then watched the floor as if my presence were too much.
And in the silence, the white men moved,
their pockets full of time, their steps so sure
cushioned by what they stole.
'They steal my time, I shall not last much longer.'
And I protested, unconvinced, for you had aged so much.
And who could say what they forced out of you
behind those walls. The essence maybe of our time,
dripping so slowly in our blood.
Maybe they stole the measure. (ibid.:19)

Like Oedipus' daughter, this speaker also considers the possibility that enlightenment may well emerge from those cast out of the familiar social context. After all, Oedipus the outcast bestowed the most powerful guiding myth of Western civilisation, although the nature of the guidance may still contain unexplored interpretive possibilities (Olivier,1989). The last line of the stanza quoted above re-echoes in the opening stanza of the title poem of the second collection, and offers one possible gloss on 'measure':

To find our measure, exactly,
not the echo of other voices.
The present growing out of our lungs
like a flower, with a smell
that we have re-traced through our veins
some dark, secret smell

that will bloom when the hour has struck
an animal smell
reminiscent of blood
the world's scent. (Kefala, 1978:8)

In this poem a 'we' is established as firmly bonded by a communal experience of 'foreignness'. The first part explores a disjunction between subjects and place; all are reduced to shadows. The second part moves once again into the alternative realities of madness. The 'you' of 'Memory' echoes in the words, 'They were stealing your time'. The mark of madness settles silently, disguising blood as golden powder, the inner nightmare still contained by the ordered daily self. Part three recalls the dark room and disruptive 'foreign laugh' of 'Memory', but fleshes out in further detail the encroaching hallucinations which manifest themselves in 'the silent room'. In the outside world the counterpoint hymn to Mary carries an undercurrent of menace in its appellation, 'Siren of the Waters', and in its 'chorus of women, black clad'. The 'new' religion barely contains the old. Part four follows the stricken emissary to the nightmare house which contains gorgons' heads and the message 'The virgin they had hidden'. The old forces appear to have triumphed, though the nature of their victory is only hinted at: 'the mirrors everywhere/blooming relentlessly, pools of white fire/unable to contain the unimagined' (ibid.:11).

The final part offers images of 'the ring' and menacing 'nets' which evoke the bloodthirsty world of the *Oresteia*, or even older orders. The 'you' is enmeshed in sacrificial rituals, and the earlier allusions to light and fire culminate in the image of 'fire worshippers' and 'thirsts no air could cure'. The final stanza, akin to the end of 'Memory', observes the troubled 'you' caught in an obsessive search for water; the mechanised miming of actions strips them of their familiar meanings, as in the behaviour of the dying and the insane.

The effect of the poem is to suggest an intensely personal but completely private experience. The details bring it to vivid life but do not evoke specific individuals; we never even know the nature of the bond between the narrator and the protagonist. The movement at the end recalls the Lacanian concept of aphanisis—the fading of the subject (Lacan, 1977a:216–29; 1977b:283–4). When the myths are withdrawn and social rituals no longer signify, when possible selves proliferate, there arises a fear of inundation, of not emerging as a subject at all, and being unable to sustain subjectivity.[3] This situation is rendered most graphically in the title poem 'The Alien' (Kefala, 1973:20). It surfaces also in 'Farewell Party' ('my shape was going from me/while I watched it', Kefala, 1978:42), in a section about the Eumenides, who are the chthonic goddesses of (perhaps) a matriarchal era in which blood ties and the rights of the mother and of the earth dominated in law.

Kefala's poetry constructs a writing subject for whom the use of words is not a reassuring entry into the social but, rather, a journey on to a tightrope with no safety nets—as, for example, in her poem 'The Acrobat' (Kefala, 1973:11). It is a process, moreover, where visibility in the public world is too often confined to the execution of clever tricks, and to the loss of a darkness and silence which offer other, and perhaps shattering, possibilities.

The family constellation, so often a ghetto of solidarity in realist migrant writing (see Lewitt, 1980, 1985 for fine examples of this genre), is here breached and vulnerable, and offers no protection:

> I am tired, living at home among strangers,
> sitting at the same tables,
> waiting for an acceptance that never comes,
> an understanding that would not be born,
> the measure in us already spent. (Kefala, 1973:8)

The family group disperses into individuals isolated by not being 'interpellated' or hailed into social identity (Althusser, 1976). A much later poem on this theme is set within the context of a return to Europe, but here too the family proffers no help: 'Marble dusted, ancient faces/with eroded eyes,/shell eyes of statues bleached by time' (Kefala, 1988a:19). The eyes offer no reflection, no confirmation. In Lacanian psychoanalysis it is the terrain and gaze of the Other which consolidates the subject. The Other may consist of the social in many forms: the mother, language, a range of signifying systems.

While Kefala's novellas explore gender roles in some detail, the poetry does so only sporadically. As in the case of Walwicz's work, discussed below, gender roles are depicted as masks, costumes, and charades. For example, 'At the Pictures' offers a disturbingly cannibalistic spectacle of the traditional young couple:

> They had started the evening together,
> waiting in their seats, the girl silent,
> the boy noisy, with curly hair,
> his busy hands touching her hungrily,
> like a thirsty man who would never
> have enough, eating her away, diligently,
> absorbed, with vacant eyes.
> The hunger not his, passed on,
> untouched, from the beginning,
> inhabiting shadows. (Kefala, 1973:16)

The shadows contain the lurking gods who often inhabit the wings in Kefala's work, and who enact in this example their traditional rites of possession. The comment on heterosexual traditions is clear and devastating.

In 'Concert' elderly women perform their allotted role as bearers of culture, 'powdered white . . . suspended . . . in ether' (ibid.:9), just as in other poems women are represented as 'staging' their femininity (Kefala, 1978:26, 50). Pathetically anachronistic, these votaries are, like their culture, slightly out of place. The final stanza, however, transfigures them and gives renewed significance to their own 'promised land' and 'unseen god'. A different kind of elderly woman appears in 'The Women in Black', sustained by another kind of faith—Christian but linked also with older gods who inhabit other poems (ibid.:22). Such figures (women in black) are rooted in the earth and are in touch with its chthonic powers. The later work links the 'lady herself' of the Christian pantheon with these other goddesses:

> The evening was falling
> on the porcelain dust
> that moved on the waters
> the milky white breath
> of the goddess with snakes

who travelled below
her slim arms outstretched
poised at the centre
a secretive smile
on her listening mouth.

At her feet
the octopus waited
watchful
with eyes of the deep. (Kefala, 1988a:18)

After all, others have also seen a connection between pre-Christian snake goddesses and the traditional icon of Mary standing on the serpent.

The two poems which conclude *Thirsty Weather* offer the convergence of a series of places from which the writing subject has been speaking in the course of each of the first two volumes. In 'Epilogue' (Kefala, 1978:52), there is a collective 'we' moving like lost souls or Homeric shadows in the limbo of 'long medicinal rooms'. For ethnic minority readers whose presence is not yet acknowledged within mainstream Australian culture, this is a poignant image. The lurking insanity depicted in 'Memory' and 'Thirsty Weather' haunts all those who have been uprooted from the signifying systems which gave them meanings. In the final poem, 'The Hour', a dreaming narrator witnesses the silent murder of another alien people, culturally identified by the reference to 'greenstone tongues' (ibid.:53). The image of Maori suffering is juxtaposed with Tiresias, the bisexual poet and seer who is then linked with the narrator.

Kefala is not the first ethnic minority writer to seek affinity with other silenced voices (Gunew,1987b). It is interesting to see how she taps the pre-colonial mythic darkness of New Zealand and links it with her own cultural legacy in order to construct, via dreams, a new language of myth. Both individual and at the same time impersonal, Kefala's poetry constructs fragments of migrant subjects which draw the attention of some Australian readers to a 'foreignness' with which they should be more familiar. To other Australians, aware of their hyphenated cultural affiliations, she signals 'a new measure'. More recently, Kefala's work has finally generated analyses informed by contemporary post-structuralist criticism and the debates around modernity (Hatzimanolis, 1990; Papastergiadis, 1992).

Broadly speaking, Ania Walwicz's prose poems reproduce or re-enact the linguistic and social contradictions which construct any subject. Walwicz, a very different kind of writer, approaches language by replicating its semi- or unconscious shaping powers: hence the incantatory and repetitious style of her texts. Not surprisingly, given its overtly experimental style, Walwicz's work has had a reception history very different from but no less troubled than Kefala's (Walwicz, 1992b). For example, she is continually taken to task for techniques which clearly derive from high modernism—stream of consciousness, automatic writing, dream sequences, and so on. None the less, she is constantly ridiculed for these quite traditional ways of marking experimental or avant-garde writing. She has frequently situated herself not only in a literary tradition evolving from Gertrude Stein (Gibbs, 1989–90) but also from popular culture such as rock music (and particularly icons such as Elvis Presley). Because she is a charismatic performer of her own work, this has also been construed as a limitation: it has been said, for instance, that the work literally requires her voice in order to convey its full meaning (Walwicz, 1992b:821–2). This marks a particularly vulgar manifestation of the notion of authorial presence as a sustaining device in literature.

Ania Walwicz arrived in Australia from Poland in 1963 at the age of thirteen. Her prose poems adopt, in the main, a parodic mode. Recurrent motifs include cultural dislocation, and gender conceived as a continuum rather than as the fixed opposition of sexual difference. In that area of her writing which deals specifically with the migrant experience, she has fashioned a powerful trope which reduces adult migrants to children (Walwicz, 1982a:34–5; 1982b:84; in Gunew 1981:2). Terms depicting childhood often function also to indicate social hierarchies or class differences (Ariès, 1979:24); and in Walwicz's world of power inversions, adults shrink to children, while children are forced to become the caretakers of their own parents. Another significant device in her work is parody of the so-called 'broken English' of immigrants. Walwicz's poetry is characterised by simple language and hypnotic repetitions well suited to performance poetry, and her performance skills may be sampled in the record included with the anthology called *Off the Record* (Π. O., 1985). The prevailing associative logic is familiar to us from dreams, or, at least, from traditions of surrealist writing. Displacement and condensation are the governing devices: similar words and contiguous words structure the poems.

> Displacement involves the transfer of psychic intensity from an unacceptable element to an acceptable one, while condensation effects the formation of a new signifier from a cluster of previous signifying materials. In other words, the first of these agencies neutralizes the differences between two similar contiguous things by asserting their emotional equivalence, while the second achieves the same thing by insisting on their absolute coincidence. (Silverman, 1983:89)

A cluster of Walwicz's poems deals with first contacts with the new culture, and offers variations on the trope of parent–child reversals. The parents grow increasingly smaller under the pressures of alien social processes and rely on their children to negotiate the social apparatus. The children, in time, disappear under this burden as, for example, in 'so little':

> We were so big there and could do everything. When you have lots you know it. Lucky and lucky and money. My father was the tallest man in the world. Here we were nothing. There vet in the district and respect. The head of the returned soldiers and medals. Here washed floors in the serum laboratory. Shrinking man. I grow smaller every day. The world gets too big for me. We were too small for this big country. We were so little. We were nothing. We were none and naught and no money. We were no speak. There we were big and big time. Here we were so little. Hardly any. We grew tiny. Scared lost not knowing how to speak. At the mercy of other people to put us up. We didn't amount to much. There I was good at school. Here they put me in a grade lower. We grew smaller in height. We were reduced. We had a smaller area. Before we had a house. And here we had only one room to be in. I had big ideas before and here I didn't know how to say what I wanted to be. Was no one and nothing

at all. I didn't belong anywhere. I was hardly here. Waiting for people to pick me up after school. And I forgot my address and wouldn't know what to say to anybody. And if they didn't pick me up I'd stand there all night and wouldn't know what to do at all. I was so small. The shower was too big for me. When you have plenty you can be kind. Father goes away. Mother goes away. They had room to move. Now we didn't have any. We were put in a box. We are so poor and all together. I used to think how nice that could be. But it wasn't nice. And we were at one another. We turned on one another. And quarrelled. And I ran away. And he ran away. And I didn't go to school one day. And we went to the golf links. And sat on a bench and escaped. And I got a cold and stayed in bed. And I was unhappy. And we were lost. And he could not do his job. And had to pass exams. And we didn't have any money. And the landlord came. Two little girls hid under the bed. He saw through the window and felt sorry. I had to be old early and ashamed of what happened. We are going to travel he said. Your name will be Anne. Your name will be Mary. I was hoping they'd catch us near the border. But they didn't. And we travelled in the white snow that was nowhere. And in the blue ocean that was nowhere. To get to a place where we were less and had less and were less and less and grew smaller every day. (Walwicz, 1983:19)

The poem begins by invoking the childhood fantasy that parents, particularly fathers, are all-powerful and confer these privileges, by extension, on the whole family ('We were so big there and could do everything'). In the oneiric logic of condensation, the shrinking father shrinks the child narrator. Words structure reality, as in Freud's analysis of dreams, where words are treated 'as if they were things, with all the same affective and sensory properties' (Silverman, 1983:84). Social impotence means literally to shrink in size and progressively to fade away (the reference is to aphanisis); loss of speech is equated with loss of existence. Within their alien environment the migrant subjects progressively dissolve: from 'tallest . . . in the world' to being confined in a house, then a room, a box, to hiding under the bed, to nothing ('the white snow that was nowhere'). Even names, those potent signifiers of social identity, disappear: this is a common motif in ethnic minority writing that is specifically migrant writing.

In 'Poland' (Walwicz, 1982a:37) memories of the previous culture are rapidly transformed into a total fabrication: 'child stories', stories told by a child and to a child. Again meaning is dependent on words organised at a literal level: memory, like a piece of cloth, fades and then unravels. Those who have gone 'over the horizon line' have died. Initially, the link is provided by dreams ('I went back every night'), but when these are not confirmed by the daily life, the past place and the past self disappear. Poland becomes 'Poland', simply a place on the map which one reads about in the papers. Poland may be said to function as the 'lost object' of psychoanalysis:

> The erotogenic zones or somatic gaps become the points through which the child attempts to introject into itself those things which give it pleasure, and which it does not yet distinguish from itself. The first such object is generally the breast, and it is of course inserted into the orifice of the mouth . . . Other objects which enjoy the same privileged status are the faeces, and the gaze and voice of another, such as the mother. There will be many such objects in the life of the subject. Lacan refers to them as *'objets petit a '*, which is an abbreviation for the more complete formula *'objets petit autre'*. This rubric designates objects which are not clearly distinguished from the self and which are not fully grasped as other (*autre*). The object derives its value from its identification with some missing component of the subject's self, whether that loss is seen as primordial, as the result of a bodily organisation, or as the consequence of some other division. (Silverman, 1983:156)

Underlying the vehement tone of Walwicz's poem is the harrowing implication that the self constructed 'over there' in Poland has no currency in the present 'here' and 'now' in Australia: a self derived from a particular cluster of signifying systems has become irrelevant ('This is finished and finished . . . gone and is gone').

In 'wogs' (in Gunew, 1987a:133) the predicament is viewed, so to speak, from the other side. An unpunctuated, relentless chorus announces the stereotypes of prejudice familiar to immigrants.

Although it is an evocation of untutored voices, full of contradictions, it is uncannily reminiscent of certain enunciations deriving from so-called high culture. The logical momentum of the poem invokes all the standard fears associated with racism: miscegenation, alien food, skin the wrong colour, and uncontrolled breeding. All add up to the concept of 'wogs' as non-human ('dark skin monkeys'). A later poem, 'europe' (Walwicz, 1989b:71), is also based on stereotypical images from mass culture, in this case, the discourse of travelogues. The narrator, initially not gendered, catalogues European diversity metonymically and appropriately as consisting of rich food: this recurrent link between migrants, ethnic minorities and food needs to be theorised (Gunew, 1993b). There is also a hint of the pre-Oedipal and pre-linguistic child who recognises no boundaries and absorbs the world, everything, into its own body ('inside me is Europe'). As in post-war Australia, the signifier 'Europe' gestures towards an undifferentiated conglomeration of foreign countries. Once again, as at the beginning of 'Poland', there is the sense that living memory, the actual memory of Europe, displaces or is more palpable than the here and now of the new place. In this case, though, the tone is more mocking and parodic, as though the readers are being served only the clichéd concepts (if not the forms) they expect. The advent of 'carl', fresh from Europe, shifts the narrator's 'europe' back into dreams ('I ride in my first night with goblins'). The narrator labours to sustain and give back body to 'europe' as reminiscence, but is increasingly dependent on the support of artefacts such as pictures. The reference to 'soir de paris perfume my wrist' hints at gender, only to be displaced shortly afterwards by 'I'm young man' (see Silverman, 1983:158, on the 'mirror-stage' identification with the 'ideal' self in the Lacanian model of the acquisition of subjectivity). In this final mastery of 'europe' the narrator is established as male, Teutonic and full of potential ('everything is going to be').

'New World' (Walwicz, 1982a:67), the final poem in Walwicz's first collection, comprises the paradoxical celebration of a subject who is visibly there but refuses his own history. Beginning as 'Mister New' with no forebears, the narrator simultaneously refers to 'prison' and to 'hospital', possibly signalling the past which is being disavowed. Gender becomes increasingly complicated when Mister New gives birth to a new self ('I give me birth'). The male autogenesis is presumably more authoritative than the more familiar female parthenogenesis, but is then qualified by 'Thin dress . . . Joy is my name'. For those who are marked negatively by social sign systems (migrant, female), the possibility of rebirth is a compelling fantasy. It is accompanied, explicitly and implicitly, by the concept of an autonomous and originating subject. This theme is celebrated at greater length in the poem 'I': 'I am the driver . . . I am the world. There is nothing outside of me' (in Gunew, 1987a:134). Paradoxically, what is finally signalled here is that pre-symbolic stage *before* the subject develops a coherent subjectivity: the period when the child cannot distinguish between itself and the world at large.

The construction of gender in Walwicz's poetry is illuminated by Juliet Mitchell's analysis (1984:289–90) of how the hysteric refuses to line up on one side or the other of a socially constituted sexual division. Walwicz's poetry is indeed filled with this refusal. 'Masculinity' and 'femininity' are displayed as a series of poses and masquerades rather than as referring to any essential truths (Owen, 1985:7–8). For example, 'The All Male Sauna' (Walwicz, 1982a:14) begins with 'I was a little girl again', which sets the tone for a tongue-in-cheek catalogue of 'femininity' (what are little girls made of?). What is being celebrated here is the over-determined femininity associated with female impersonators, but which is, at the same time, part of a continuum of what constitutes 'normal' femininity in our own society. Many of Walwicz's poems deal with bisexuality, and a play of hers performed in Melbourne at the Anthill Theatre in January 1985 is called *Girl/boy Talk*. Also on this continuum is the Freudian notion of the fetish, succinctly described by Elizabeth Wright (1984:93) as an over-investment in something in order to cover over a lack. In 'Photos' (Walwicz, 1982a:56) anxieties engendered by the fragmented (or even non-existent) self are covered over with fetishised images. The endless taking of photos becomes a guarantee of existence, serving the recognition or hailing into being of the subject by social institutions ('So other people will look at me and see me'). Autogenesis and self-control (or control over the self) are again present. Recorded here is a series of selves—the strip of photos on the book's cover becomes teasingly contextualised. The self exists only on film fragments (or in fragmented writing), 'This comes out of me' and is unified only through the assertions of the narrator's 'I' ('I want to catch what I feel . . .This is really me'). But as we know from linguistic analysis (Silverman, 1983:185–6), the signifier 'I' has meaning only within the terms of the discourse in which it appears (for example, in relation to a 'you') and not in relation to an outside referent. Thus the repetition in the poem of 'I' perversely draws attention to the very absence that is being strenuously denied. The vehement affirmation of a unified subject puts that very concept into question.

Both the 'second childhood' motif and the fragmentation of language recur in her text 'translate' (Walwicz,1989b:83), which forms one of a trio of performance pieces on the video entitled *Europa* (Walwicz, 1987b). In his essay 'Des Tours de Babel', Derrida reminds us that the recognition of the need for translation 'ruptures the colonial violence or the linguistic imperialism' (Derrida, 1985a:174) upon which the notion of a universal language is predicated. This focuses our attention on the political aspects of entering a homogenised or unified language, where one of the values incorporated by those who arrive (the immigrants) is to remind those already there of the codes of initiation and entry (Sollors, 1986:251–2) which operate in that culture. Another value is that these immigrants affirm the identity of the dominant group by functioning, in Gayatri Spivak's (1986) terms, as self-confirming others. Migrants are constituted for sociology and oral history as unproblematic informants who deliver the putative validity of unmediated experience—that true-life story or paradigmatic narrative which consolidates the unified subject who, in turn, confirms linguistic and other imperialisms.

One of the most effective ways of upsetting such cultural imperialisms is to insert other tongues into the prevailing English idiom. Those who derive from non-Anglo cultures and languages, and are forced to negotiate a new symbolic (in Lacan's sense of the term), find that the name-of-the-father which dominates in the old symbolic has become delegitimised in the new country. In other words, since in Western culture we operate inevitably with binary oppositions (and there seems only one place for the dethroned 'father' to go) this is tantamount to arguing that the illegitimate name-of-the-father is assigned the maternal position—not simply that of the biological mother, but of that pre-symbolic realm of the semiotic, which Julia Kristeva (1980:124–47) has described as consisting of pulsions and a rhythmic babble.

In the essay on translation Derrida (1985:167) also plays with notions of legitimation, moving from the Father/God as origin of language to the plurality of mother tongues. The importance for nationalist enterprises of an original, sacred and legitimising language has often been explored (Hartman, 1980). In this case, the question Derrida poses is not simply how to convey the necessary plurality of languages but how to achieve this in translation. In the present instance, how does my own critical interpretation, which involves a translation, convey the plurality of the English and Polish? As Paul de Man puts it, 'Both criticism and translation are caught in the gesture which Benjamin calls ironic, a gesture which undoes the stability of the original by giving it a definitive, canonical form in the translation or in the theorization' (1985:35).

The Polish language in the poem functions, for those who don't understand it, as the untranslatable which is the condition of translation. It emphasises the importance of recognising both the need to translate and its inherent impossibility. It registers itself as the indigestible aspect of a vulgar multiculturalism which cannot simply be consumed as ethnic cooking, costumes or quaint customs.

The tower is built and confusion reigns: but for whom? The narrator speaks of needing to renovate her house in conjunction with painfully remembering the Polish language, the former life that she has almost forgotten. 'Self' and 'house' are familiar metonyms of one another. At the same time we are informed that the renovator, like all authority figures, will not come on call. Does this signify the lost name-of-the-father? To juxtapose this poem with the first text in the trilogy of pieces, 'dad' (Walwicz,1989b:163), renders such a reading perhaps too easy. Before that we are given the dwarf (*krasnoludek*)—possibly, again, the father reduced and refashioned as trickster, transgressively associated with pissing. This is the symbolic father returned to the semiotic space of the body criss-crossed with spasms and pulsions. The carnivalesque is also suggested by references to play and the theatre—the lost scene of childhood and language. The lost words become synonymous with old or 'tragic' toys. In an interview, Walwicz (1987a) refers to these 'tragic old toys' as being associated with war, an image of damage and cruelty to the self, and cruelty perpetrated on a child.

In the video version, the red hood and trousers of the narrator are linked with a plaster garden gnome, which visually recalls the stunted adults of other poems. Also evoked is the powerful transgressive image of an earlier poem in which little Red Riding Hood haunts the shadows, carries a knife and accosts men with, 'Want some sweeties mister?' (Walwicz, 1982:7). The child/adult as clumsy foundling sardonically re-enacts the migrant experience: the adult baby who suddenly cannot speak.

Another frame of reference for the poem (reversed of course) is that of the language class: all those after-hours English classes held in schools, in which adult immigrants are squeezed into children's desks. Here, the implied Anglo readers are put into the position of being assaulted with a language *they* cannot understand. In addition, the piece caricatures the first-person mode: the 'simple' telling of one's life story, the 'simple' identity of the migrant subject. From the assumption of authority in the language lesson, the narrator moves to explore other advantages in having access to another language. The 'foreigner has some extra'. Whether by being able to discuss other people openly on a tram, or having the knowledge of another country in the back of their heads, migrants are emphatically not defined through lack: neither the lack of English nor its supposed corollary, the lack of cultural plenitude.

The poem begins, 'inne different'—the absence of difference precedes the acquisition of language with its concomitant assumption of subjectivity. The subject cannot return to a pre-linguistic self. In the video version we are given the shot of a pickled tongue. The old tongue cannot simply be pickled, though this makes for good eating. Walwicz's work continues to confound expectations concerning ethnic minority writings. More generally, her experimental style—equally marked in her first novel *red roses* (Walwicz, 1992a)—continues to antagonise reviewers like Oakley (1992:8) and Davison (1992). But Walwicz's writings are now attracting sustained academic analysis (Jacobson,1990; Gillett, 1991) in ways that as yet Kefala's have not.

The Grotesque Migrant Body: Rosa Cappiello's *Oh Lucky Country*

No, vorrei mettere una bomba in culo all'Australia e poi andare a vendere giornali tra le rovine. Ridi? Ridi, ridi. Tu ti adegui. Ti nutri a scopate secche leggendo libri. Ti sazi di parole mute. Io non ci riesco. Io non reggo questo deserto. Io crollo. (Cappiello, 1981:54)

I'd like to stick a bomb up Australia's arsehole and then go sell papers among the ruins. You're laughing, are you? Well, go ahead and laugh. You adapt yourself. You get by on dry fucks by reading books. You stuff yourself with dumb words. I can't take it. I can't bear this wasteland. I'm going to pieces. (Cappiello, 1984:52–3)

There are no stiff upper lips in Rosa Cappiello's *Oh Lucky Country*, no Anglo-ethnic understatements. In fact there are no stiff or solid boundaries anywhere in this novel, which inflates migrant oppression to such absurdist proportions that in its very excessiveness it becomes a force for renewal and imaginative energy. Cappiello, an immigrant from Naples, initially wrote the book in Italian. Unfortunately, as the introduction by the translator Gaetano Rando informs us, readers of the English version miss out on the word play and allusions which draw upon the Neapolitan dialect as well as on Italo-Australian inflections. But readers of the English version certainly hear a new voice in Australian writing, wickedly parodic:

Anzac day is a great national holiday, a day for lots of drinking. Dusty ghosts who resurrect the martyrs of the past, no longer with us, kaput, and, after the parade, when cannon, machine guns, flags, patriotic speeches are all wrapped up and put away, the wankers rush off to the pub to wash the residue of desert dust out of their throats. For me it is a day of rest, a different day from the usual, a day which makes the migrant feel part and parcel of the system, you can be patriotic in any country, and it is a comforting feeling to admire the brand new weapons as they file through the opening formed by the compact crowd and to think of what could burst forth from that pacific and bedecked ironmongery should it rush to the front in our defence . . . (ibid.:76–7)

In so far as we hear migrant or ethnic minority voices at all in Australian writing, we are accustomed to hearing them as victims, doubly enhanced by the first-person mode. These accounts, duly reworked into the muted understatements acceptable to Anglo-Celtic ears, evoke a pity tinged with complacency. Mainstream readers are not prepared for this kind of extravaganza in which outcast voices from the gutter, from the bottom of the heap, boil over into a flood which sweeps away many clichés about being a migrant:

Together with the migrant masses I am contributing to the process of your civilization, to widening your horizon which doesn't extend any further than the point of your great ugly nose. I tear the weeds out of your ears. I give you a certain style. I teach you to eat, to dress, to behave and above all not to belch in restaurants, trains, buses, cinemas, schools. You probably don't know, but I'll tell you in confidence, for your information, that your country, which is now mine too, is based on a gigantic belch. Its flag flutters in the wind created by the toxic gases produced by your stomachs which are choked up like sewers. The myth about being happy and lucky is based on your drunken bouts. Go on, then, drink. You offend us. You don't like wine? You prefer beer? Waiter, a huge bottle of beer for the lady. (ibid.:192–3)

So how has this book been received? Judging from the few reviews of *Oh Lucky Country*, the immediate response was to dismiss it patronisingly as incompetent:

> But the essence of the book, Rosa's feeling of alienation from the angrifying world around her, is a great starting point for a putative novelist. One can only hope that she not only maintains her rage, but now sets about learning something—anything would do—of the novelist's craft. (Macklin, 1985)

The charge of incompetence is a familiar one in reviews of works by so-called ethnic writers. The obvious response to this example is first, that the reviewer himself should learn something ('anything would do') about literary history in order to give him a context other than the realist mode in which to situate texts, and second, that he take a course in literary theory which, among other things, might teach him not to confuse the author with the narrator.

But aside from these specific flaws, this review points to the much larger problem of how migrant or ethnic minority writing is positioned *vis-à-vis* Australian literature. To position any group as marginal always turns out to be an exercise in reinforcing some putative and dominant norm; it involves oiling the machinery of legitimation rather than interrogating that whole enterprise of canonisation.

Cappiello's text employs the first-person point of view, which is so much easier to read as transparent sociology than to analyse seriously in terms of its formal textual properties. Moreover, first-person narratives facilitate those idealist or commonsense readings which perpetuate the production of unified subjects: the author, the narrator, the woman, and the migrant converge in the spurious unity of an 'I'. The text is heard as a natural, untutored confession. What would happen to this traditional unity if it were scrutinised instead in terms of postmodernist techniques? Intertextuality—the way 'books talk among themselves' (Eco, 1984:1)—should be an automatic reading strategy for those who wish to situate ethnic minority writing, and who need to be alert to culturally specific antecedents. In this case they are both Italian and Australian. Dante's *Commedia* is an inevitable, shadowy precursor. Here, for example, is an account of the bottom of the world seen from below:

> *Io levai gli occhi, e credetti vedere*
> *Lucifero com'io l'avea lasciato,*
> *e vidili le gambe in su tenere;*
> *e s'io divenni allora travagliato,*
> *la gente grossa il pensi, che non vede*
> *qual è quel punto ch'io avea passato.*

> I raised my eyes, and thought to see
> Lucifer as I had left him;
> and saw him with his legs turned upwards;
> and the gross people who see not what
> that point is which I had passed,
> let them judge if I grew perplexed then.
> (Dante, *Inferno*, XXXIV, lines 88–93)

Thus Dante and Virgil, with the coyness of high culture, look down on Lucifer ass-side up. In this space below the ass-hole of the world what can one say or write? And having produced it (and oneself in the process), how will it be heard? There are early references in Cappiello's text to the 'migrant inferno', and the narrator is called Rosa. There are roses, infernos, peripatetic narrators, guides in various guises, and always (I will return to this) invocations of the female principle—parodically inverted Beatrices and worse, as we shall see, when we arrive at Rosa's Assumption. Such connections need of course to be pursued more rigorously with the Italian original of both texts. We are dealing, after all, with a poetic prose here.

Similarly the Italo-Australian echoes (referred to by both Rando, 1984 and Schiavoni, 1982) need to be savoured in the original. But we can appreciate some of the gestures towards culturally specific Australian images. The book opens with references to the 'prison' of 'emigration rejection', the sea, King's Cross, the pub and, at more general levels, the world of outcasts and the gutter, those masses imprisoned in squalid inner-city surroundings. As in so much early Australian writing, the prison and the process of imprisonment function as organising tropes: the overcrowded rooms, the subsistence work in factory prisons, and finally (and not least) the imprisoning stories of others (Cappiello, 1984:16). These remind us that the book does not come from nowhere, and that those who read it as the confessional voice of naive suffering are telling us more about their own preconceptions of 'migrant writing' than about Cappiello's novel. But the allusions in *Oh Lucky Country* point to its literary antecedents: the text is engaged in a continual parody of high or received culture of any kind.

> This is my kingdom and I fit in like a gardenia in a dandy's buttonhole. I'm sorry I'm not a painter. If I were I'd express through my painting the trust this street inspires in me and the privilege of being able to live here. I'd paint the wretched gutter where the cat slakes its thirst, the unkempt woman who in the morning, already drunk, pops out of her filthy dressing gown to collect her bottle of milk. I'd paint the pretty Lebanese poofter with the misty eyes and the sincere smile on his lips when he says 'hello' to me. I'd paint the mothers with their little children dangling from their breasts who, without having brushed their teeth, run still sleepy to their work, the sound and the fury of that precise moment when they rush out into the street, spurred on by the chaotic hurry to free themselves of their offspring, blood polluted by cents when boiling over with pride and boasting, guts tangled in the machinery, tears without salt, faeces constipated because of a sedentary life, hands which give bitter caresses, the absurd words which they exchange when they gather together for their meal. I'd paint the feverish race for gain. The impulse which turns simple people into their own executioners. I would generate the song of songs in paint. The Apocalypse with an alarm clock in its hands. There would be no other canvas, pictures or displays at my passing. I'd mutate the flesh of the workers into paper money for bank reserves, their sweat into the ribbon which ties it, their feverish eyes into diamonds and gold nuggets as big as pin heads. With their fatigue and their suffering I'd paint the side dish to accompany their plate of minestrone, on a yellow canvas two metres by three point four. (ibid.:40)

But this too—this parodic, excessive, and disruptive writing—has its textual antecedents.

Migrants from non-English-speaking backgrounds tend to be relegated to 'honorary' working-class subject-positions, and in this respect they are excluded from certain kinds of public, authoritative discourses. Hence they are easily labelled textually incompetent. Within Australian writing there is a tradition, in spite of its vaunted egalitarianism or classlessness, of voices from underground. One thinks here of writers such as Peter Mathers or Barry Dickins and others. In the review quoted already, Macklin remarks: 'But unquestionably her wild mode of expression adds a great deal to the pulling power of the book; not only because scatology is rare among female writers but because in this work, despite its all-pervasive presence, it is so palpably honest'. This begs the question of what dishonest scatology looks like, and ignores all those other writers who summon the rhetoric of the outcast and the powerless, such as Genet, Pasolini and their forebear Rabelais.

In his study of Rabelais the Russian critic Mikhail Bakhtin (1968) develops the concepts of 'carnival' and the 'grotesque' body in relation to lower-class culture. Bakhtin theorises what he calls the grotesque body as representative of a celebratory aspect of pre-industrial popular culture which contrasts with official and classical culture. He describes this culture as non-privatised: it comprises what he terms the ancestral body, which constantly swings between death and rebirth, the one always incorporating the other. There are no boundaries or limits between the grotesque body and the world: 'The grotesque body . . . is a body in the act of becoming. It is never finished, never completed . . . Moreover, the body swallows the world and is itself swallowed by the world' (Bakhtin, 1968:317).

He characterises this marketplace culture as non-individualised and communal. Analogously, the narrator in *Oh Lucky Country* is prevented from acting and speaking as an individual by being constantly enmeshed in and inundated by the ethnic minority subculture, which in turn is attached to a (largely passive) working-class Australian culture:

Migrants live in a huge village square, or rather an immense rubbish heap, no matter what nationality they are, trapped into mouthing false repelling words which they then set free to wander from one lewd mouth to the other. A big happy family. Just like those universal preachers dream about. All joined together as though by an umbilical cord in a brotherhood of wheeling and dealing, trampling and dishonour. (Cappiello, 1984:37)

The reader who expects to encounter realist characterisation in Cappiello's depiction of this world discovers instead caricatures (spawned, in part at least, from the *commedia dell'arte*) whose qualities are exaggerated according to the precepts of a highly stylised morality. More specifically, these figures are linked with a Neapolitan folk tradition of representative grotesques (Rando, 1984; Schiavoni, 1982). As the Macklin review indicates, Cappiello's scatological style is seen as difficult to place within an English tradition, although comparisons with Swift's invective (and even with Beckett's) suggest themselves, since they share a common outraged moralism.

Bakhtin describes the grotesque body's focus on the mouth, the most important orifice for those who have no official voice: 'It dominates all else. The grotesque face is actually reduced to the gaping mouth; the other features are only a frame encasing the wide-open bodily abyss' (1968:317). It is also linked, like everything else in this dualistic world, with its opposite, the reverse face of the buttocks. These classic reversals and displacements are seen as breaking down the distinctions between high and low, sacred and profane culture, thus demolishing hierarchies of power and the more metaphysical hierarchies of birth and death. The upper and lower face give birth to new bodies, including new discourses, new textualities, often in the form of invective or abuse. Swearing is always directed at someone, and so this mode always addresses a generalised 'you'. But neither the speaker nor addressee of this kind of dialogue is individualised; there is simply 'voice'. In Cappiello the 'I' often dissolves into this representative voice.

Weigh me down with your excreta, your hates, your fights, your wretched little quarrels, and I shall take them all in and make them bear fruit. Everything that lies buried in the depths of your stinking carcasses, sex, murder, song and gangrene, that travels in the hinterland and the wide-open universes, I take it all in. (Cappiello, 1984:49)

This is reminiscent of Bakhtin's words on the imperative to produce dialogue, 'For discourse (and therefore, for man) nothing is more frightening than the *absence of answer*' (Bakhtin in Todorov, 1984:111).

In order to analyse in greater detail the kinds of invective used in the text and their relation to the enunciating subject, it helps to refer here to Bakhtin's (1968:427) notion of the 'blazon', which comprises lists of attributes remaining 'outside the official system of straight and strict evaluations. They were a free and ambiguous praise-abuse'. Furthermore, 'this style is characterised by the absence of neutral words and expressions. It is colloquial speech, always addressed to somebody' (ibid.:420).

The dual tone never wants to halt the spinning wheel, to find and outline the top and the bottom, the front and the back; on the contrary, it marks their continuous change and fusion. In popular speech the accent is always placed on the positive element (but we repeat, without tearing it away from the negative). In the official philosophy of the ruling classes such a dual tone of speech is, generally speaking, impossible: hard, well-established lines are drawn between all the phenomena (and these phenomena are torn away from the contradictory world of becoming, of the whole). A monotone character of thought and style almost always prevails in the official spheres of art and ideology. (ibid.:432–3).

There is constant reference in Cappiello's text (1984:120–1) to this praise-abuse pattern, flights of fancy nourished by imagery of the sewer. In his later writings Bakhtin developed (out of his notion that speech is always addressed to someone) the concept of the 'dialogic' and polyphonic modes, together with the related concept of a self balanced by a necessary other. That is to say, any social dialogue inevitably begins within the self by imagining oneself outside the self:

> I cannot do without the other; I cannot become myself without the other; I must find myself within the other, finding the other in me (mutual reflection and perception). Justification cannot be justification of oneself, confession cannot be confession of oneself. I receive my name from the other, and this name exists for the other . . . *I* hides in the *other* and in *others*; it wants to be but another for others, to fully penetrate the world of others as another, and heave aside the weight of an *I* unique in the word (the *I-for-myself*). (Bakhtin in Todorov, 1984:96–7, and particularly ch. 5)

Bakhtin moved from the carnivalesque and the dialogue between classes to investigate the disruption of the unified subject in his studies of Dostoievsky (Bakhtin, 1984). His dualistic subject (self/other) is more unified than the decentred self encountered in deconstructionist and psychoanalytic theories such as Kristeva's (1984) subject-in-process. But there are similarities none the less between Bakhtin's 'self and other' and classic Lacanian analyses of the stages of subjectivity: the mirror-stage, castration and the entry into the symbolic order and into language.

Bakhtin sees the carnivalesque as functioning to give back to those who are not authorised to speak some kind of articulate solidarity; it is a discursive strategy of subversion and comic disruption. The body of the people translates into speech of the body, and operates with particular vehemence in a culture where the body exists but does not speak. Cappiello's text sutures the suppressed and marginalised body of the ethnic minority to the communal and grotesque body of Australian popular culture, and returns both to speech. In carnival the world is turned upside down; where better to locate it, then, than in the antipodes? It also signals the reign of the body instead of the spirit. What better way to give philosophical respectability to Australia's much-vaunted devotion to hedonism? Monstrous excess rules; the last shall be first, including ethnic minorities and women. One should bear in mind, on the other hand, Todorov's (1984:79–80) objection that the carnival operates only as a safety valve whose function is to reinforce hierarchical power structures.

When considering the treatment of gender in *Oh Lucky Country*, ideas drawn from the study of pre-industrial popular culture are again helpful. In an essay entitled 'Women on Top', Natalie Zemon Davis (1978) looks at 'unruly women' and symbolic sex reversals in the popular festivals, carnivals, and street life of pre-industrial Europe. Her argument is that neither of these disruptive elements serves merely to confirm traditional power hierarchies, but that instead each keeps alive the possibilities for alternative distributions of power, including the deployment of power within the family itself. 'Play with the various images of women on top', she concludes, 'kept open an alternative way of conceiving the family structure' (ibid.:172). She observes that:

> In fact the donning of female clothes by men and the adopting of female titles for riots were surprisingly frequent in the early modern period . . . The males drew upon the sexual power and energy of the unruly woman and on her license (which they had long assumed at carnival and games) to promote fertility, to defend the community's interests and standards, and to tell the truth about unjust rule. (ibid.:178, 182)

Cappiello's book teems with unruly women, from the lesbian couple at the opening (who cause a riot in the hostel) to the narrator herself and her extended female coterie. All the women are unruly; they all curse in technicolour, and none acts out a traditional sex role. Just as it overturns familiar migrant-distress stories, *Oh Lucky Country* abounds with gender reversals, beginning at the level of language in ways that readers of the English translation can only barely appreciate. According to Schiavoni,

> the novel contains a whole series of images related in meaning and in sound to the richly expressive idiom 'incazzato' which means 'angry'. *[Oh] Lucky Country* is in many ways the work of an enraged woman, an 'incazzato'. This is semantically contradictory, as we have a feminine adjective based on a phallic image (the central part of the word). Starting from this word,

which can be said to condition the narrator's very way of experiencing anger, the author consciously or unconsciously produces a rich and effective cluster of related phallic and masculine images. The important point is that in this novel a woman's anger is conveyed through phallic images and through phonetically-related expressions. (Schiavoni, 1982:8)

Gender inversions (particularly female to male) abound, both explicitly and implicitly. In addition there is a constant emphasis on inscriptions of feminine excess, thus suggesting that this is an excess inscribed within femininity itself as constructed in our culture. Recurrent images of such excess are the grotesque mouth and the grotesque womb. To explain further the way in which unruly women disrupt and overturn the ordered patterns of both society and language, it is necessary to move on from Bakhtin to the theories of Julia Kristeva. Given that Kristeva (1980:64–91) has written about Bakhtin, this is not an arbitrary shift. Bakhtin's formulations concerning carnival and the grotesque body have affinities with Kristeva's concepts of the semiotic and what she calls the 'chora', that space of pre-Oedipal drives, oral and anal, pulsions and instincts:

Discrete quantities of energy move through the body of the subject who is not yet constituted as such and, in the course of his development, they are arranged according to the various constraints imposed on this body—always already involved in a semiotic process—by family and social structures. In this way the drives, which are 'energy' charges as well as 'physical' marks, articulate what we call the chora: a nonexpressive totality is formed by the drives and their stases in a motility that is as full of movement as it is regulated . . . Our discourse—all discourse—moves with and against the chora in the sense that it simultaneously depends upon and refuses it. Although the chora can be designated and regulated, it can never be definitively posited: as a result one can situate the chora and, if necessary, lend it a topology, but one can never give it axiomatic form . . . Drives involve pre-Oedipal semiotic functions and energy discharges that connect and orient the body to the mother. (Kristeva, 1984:24–5)

Lacan has argued that the child's entry into the order of language is synonymous with its entry into the symbolic order and its submission to the law of the father. Kristeva, on the other hand, emphasises the stages preceding this entry, and argues that there remains within our experience of language (and ourselves) an earlier pre-linguistic experience which is tied to our memories of the maternal body. Labelled the semiotic, this stage is characterised by the physical aspects of language—sound, shape, rhythm—and contrasts with the notion of language as a means of ordering the self and experience rationally. From the perspective of the semiotic, there is no coherent and unified sense of identity.

To some extent derivative from Bakhtin's description of carnivalesque subversions, Kristeva's examples deal with the ways in which the semiotic (figuratively linked to maternal anarchy) erupts into the symbolic (figuratively the place of paternal law) in avant-garde writings, suspending and fragmenting the traditional transcendental subject derived from classic humanism. In Kristeva's terms, Cappiello's text could be described as organised semiotically rather than symbolically, given its reliance on jokes, exaggeration, rhythm and invective, and its disregard of sequential realist narrative structure. Certainties dissolve in this cacophany of language: 'with the act of migration we had ordered ourselves a fine funeral for our identities' (Cappiello, 1984:5). Hence the loss of the symbolic order and a unified identity. The search for new coherence is figured metonymically in Cappiello's text as the quest for money, often at the expense of children:

> This is the female factory worker, wife of the modern coolie and coolie herself, who has got down to a fine art the act of tying her baby to the bed or to the downpipe of the kitchen sink so as not to forego the happy hour on Friday which is pay day. Slave of the dollar, she sends her newly-born babe to relatives in Egypt, Yugoslavia, Spain, Greece, and after a few years back it comes like a postal package by sea or by air . . . (ibid.:14)

> Most of them deny themselves the satisfaction of bearing a child and living a quiet life just to procreate dollars. Children ruin the budget. At lunch a couple of mothers-in-waiting sit together at the table. I don't look at them. If I do I lose my appetite. They're

having a lively discussion about the cost of foetuses. The women in an advanced state of pregnancy is downcast and depressed, she says that an abortion would only have cost her three hundred dollars and that it was a big mistake not to have got rid of the child. (ibid.:29)

The style here brings to mind not only those modernist writers privileged by Kristeva (Joyce, Mallarmé, and Lautréamont) but also those archaic texts bristling with gnomic riddles and lists that one finds, for example, in pre-Christian Celtic writing (Mercier, 1969). Although one might argue that the coherence (or monologic, to go back to Bakhtin) of the symbolic order is illustrated in these ancient texts by the prevalence of extensive genealogies (dreary feats of bardic memory), this is balanced by the many appearances of unruly women possessed of gargantuan mouths and bladders.

Analogously, one could establish the existence of the decorously symbolic in Cappiello's text by examining its intertextual relations with other books, and observing its affirmation of acknowledged cultural conventions and of other texts deriving from ethnically specific antecedents. These are gestures, as one would expect, towards a multiple readership (Sollors, 1986:247ff.) of Australians, Italians and Italo-Australians, although it appears that the Italo-Australian community has treated Cappiello none too kindly (Cappiello, 1987; Rizzo, 1992).

That multiple readership is possibly made up of women, for there are no fixed gender inscriptions in the text, but only a fluid deployment of 'male' and 'female' characteristics to a range of 'male' and 'female' characters. Thus in the following passage the narrator glosses 'woman' with 'hysteric' and then displaces both with the act of writing:

What does it mean to be a woman? I get hysterical, hysteria, womb, weakness. Crap. Haven't I more strength and character than thousands of maggot males put together? There, if I were only cunning, with it, and had a degree in Anthropology or some such, I'd throw myself into an article by some famous old male writer who lets himself rave on about feminism just to get rid of the complex created by the fact that a woman can have ten orgasms to the male's single desolate one. This morning I'm feeling rather jumpy. Thanks to Lella who has upset my solitary routine, or the book I read last night which has got me up in arms. A book written in the first person where the male writer fucks all over the place making abundant use of nymphomaniacs, and all sorts of women good and bad, just to fill his six hundred pages, which is a waste because had he condensed it all to ten pages it would have turned out a masterpiece. To my mind there is nothing more effeminate and ridiculous than a man who writes, especially a man who collects the Nobel prize for literature by writing about women. All through the day while working the heavy sewing machine I think about the book I'd write. (Cappiello, 1984:88–9)

As Juliet Mitchell observes:

The woman novelist must be an hysteric. Hysteria is the woman's simultaneous acceptance and refusal of the organisation of sexuality under patriarchal capitalism. It is simultaneously what a woman can do both to be feminine and to refuse femininity, within patriarchal discourse. And I think that is exactly what the novel is; I do not believe there is such a thing as female writing, a 'woman's voice'. There is the hysteric's voice which is the woman's masculine language (one has to speak 'masculinely' in a phallocentric world) talking about feminine experience. (Mitchell, 1984:288–9)

Elsewhere, through the mouths of others as well as in her own voice, the narrator sees herself as perverse and oppositional. She signals her desire for power and for individuality with rebellious masculine imagery: 'I go back on my tracks, hands deep in my pockets. Virile thoughts whirl round in my head. Masculine thoughts also' (Cappiello, 1984:64). Her desire to escape from the undifferentiated world of her migrant peers is consistently described in masculine images. At the same time men are assigned female images. Usually they relate to impotence and the sense of passivity, but not simply that 'he was the evergreen womb which constantly sprouted snake-skin belts, crocodile-skin bags, provisions for the four season' (ibid.:209).

In *Oh Lucky Country* patriarchal power is partially undermined by the fact that women are consistently the bearers of phallic power. For example, one of the traditional bastions of patriarchy is the concept of virginity—the intact womb penetrated only by the rightful owner to produce legitimate descendants. Here is the narrator on this topic:

> Rumours were rife about the imminent landing of a thousand or so Cypriot virgins complete with medical certification in their suitcases, irrefutable proof of their purity and sentimental sincerity. It seems that the Southern European men had been complaining about not being able to find a virgin bride. The stupid men had rushed en masse to telephone, make arrangements with the newspapers, consulates, committees, priests. A tidal wave which stunned everyone. Ah, women, little did you know the value of an intact womb here in Australia as we approach the twenty-first century. Many of the women were kicking themselves because they hadn't had their virginity surgically restored. When that black hole was being discussed, that sacred hole put up for auction, a wave of homicidal rage would sweep over me. (ibid.:11–12)

Subsequently we encounter a host of 'patched up virgins' who have no trouble deceiving the representative male, 'prick eternally in hand'. The Virgin herself (and here we enter a world of complex Catholic intertextuality) is constantly dethroned both explicitly and implicitly. Parody often results:

> My second Christmas. I am still suspended in uncertainty. Couldn't be any more broken-down than I am. My liver's fit to burst. The balls which have taken the place of my ovaries too. I've had it up to here with faeces, bile, trickery, exploitation, cowardice, barely sufficient but secure wages. Christmas. Prevent the Child from being born. I am the Christ become old and rusty on the nails. Prophet of evil. Christ gone wrong. An artificial abortion. In retaliation I eliminate His mother, the Holy Virgin Mary, egging her on to revolt against Father, Son and Holy Ghost. I dress her in skirts with such daring slits which show yet do not show what is underneath. (ibid.:107)

By contrast with this explicitness, indirect parody is possibly more interesting, because what supplants the Virgin is, as one would expect, the goddess as whore, made manifest in one of her most archaic incarnations, the pig goddess of Celtic tradition (Markale, 1975:93–103). The Great Whore is the presiding deity of *Oh Lucky Country* and possesses each of the major women on various occasions. For example, there is Sofia, one of the most cunning manipulators of the system:

> Yes, our friends work at and exploit many trades, midwives, prostitutes, saints, pizza cooks, messenger girls, bankers, con-artists, greengrocers . . . Sofia is their founder. A sow in heat. She lets out her ample breath, attracting to her lap the Opera House, Ayers Rock, the Kwinana Freeway, Koala, Kangaroo, Emu, the Three Sisters, the Great Barrier Reef and fourteen million Australians. A superhuman task for anyone but not for her. (Cappiello, 1984:18–19)

Again there is the eruption of the grotesque mouth/womb. Sofia is the only one actually named after the goddess, since her real name turns out to be Concetta Prochetti (ibid.:185). Her friend Beniamina, also described on several occasions as a sow, seemingly capitulates to the patriarchal order—to marriage and to the making of money. But consider this passage:

> She no longer eats meat, her fibrous physique can't stand it, yet she doesn't refuse Claudia's steak. Coffee contains caffeine, strains the heart, so she recycles the used coffee grounds which should be thrown away. In the bathroom torn up magazines are hung on a nail instead of toilet paper, no more deodorant to get rid of the smell of the windowless bathroom, nor sea-blue liquid in the cistern, nor Baygon against the cockroaches teeming in the cupboards. She takes a bath once a week with bran, cuts cotton wool out of sanitary napkins . . . the tepid piss which comes out she drinks for tea. In the morning she squeezes her tits to obtain a drink of milk. She wrings vitamins out of mice. Reads by the light of the street lamp on the corner. (ibid.:120–1)

Beniamina saves and is avaricious in cosmic proportions, in carnivalesque excess, particularly when compared to her more mundane migrant sisters. Beniamina signifies the grotesque body in those specifically female terms explored in Kristeva's notion of abjection (see in particular Creed, 1986). She becomes pregnant, but in a manner reminiscent of an immaculate conception, since the father is one of that army of English and Australian men consistently described as drunk and impotent. Although phallic women don't by any means overthrow the phallic order, the patriarchal family relations are constantly mocked.[1] Not even the incest taboo is respected. In so far as we encounter any family it is constituted in metaphoric incest through the figure of Zio (Uncle) Lino, 'Zio Lino—Uncle Lino. A family relationship conceived in bed' (Cappiello, 1984:19).

Uncle Lino trails his harem of 'nieces' through the book and is also the owner of the 'evergreen womb' mentioned earlier. Lawful heterosexual union is further undermined by the numerous lesbian relationships encountered in the book. Nowhere do either traditional gender roles or traditional family relations prevail. The major female figures swing wildly back and forth along the masculine–feminine continuum, and so continually interrogate gender norms. Possibly the most explicit example of this gender fluidity occurs when the narrator becomes imprisoned by an Italian couple who wish to hire her as a surrogate mother. Momentarily she is trapped by her biological destiny (the price of a full stomach is a full womb), but in a fine carnivalesque sequence her female friends storm to the rescue:

> As soon as I saw them get off the truck, some holding clubs, some brooms, I leant out of an upstairs window inciting them to revolution, mayhem and massacre. My God, I could hardly believe that this army of furious women were my friends and had come to save me. (ibid.:135)

Here are unruly women with a vengeance, and here is one moment when the lucky country is depicted as neither inferno nor purgatory.

Let me end with an image which relates to the opening and the closing of this text. At the beginning the narrator focuses her disillusionment with the country on the absence of 'a time-worn grey-stone urinal in some corner of a public square' (ibid.:1), a grotesque symbol of civilisation and history. At the end, disdaining such constraints, the narrator (Rosa's Assumption) becomes the avatar for the Great Whore and releases a second flood:

> Am I perhaps a slave bought in chains and with rings in her nose, that they think they can piss on me? By all the devils in hell and all the demons in my head, by Christ and the most Holy Madonna, by all the false saints in paradise, I invoke the fights of man and all humanity. I have stored up so much of that piss over these wretched years that I could piss down from the top of the wall for centuries on end and unleash a second flood of biblical proportions. The truth of the matter is that my piss is priceless, piss streaked with blood and cancer, piss that asks no quarter, not to run to waste because in its flight it curves like a colour-changing rainbow and paints cities, plains, mountains, rivers, lakes and seas. Gather the sparkling fluid in buckets, bins, baths, troughs. A woman who has suffered too much and has learnt to piss for want of any better consolation offers it to you as a gift. (ibid.:233–4)

She ushers in a new world with (what else?) a carnival clown mask which bows to history old and new: 'and so I shortened my hair convict style and stuck a carnation over my ear' (ibid.:235).

To read this text as the outpourings of a simple soul or as transparent sociology is misdirected, for this is no unrehearsed first-person chronicle:

> But it will end, I know it will, and all this will not have happened, because what has happened and continues to happen belongs to too many people and to recognize oneself in all of this is impossible. (ibid.:236)

The king of the carnival is here the queen of the underworld. To appreciate the complexities of the discourses which produce us we must extend our reading to include not merely those multicultural others who are assimilated invariably to reinforce an 'I' we already know, but also those multicultural differences constituted by an always elusive series of 'yous'.

Homeland, Nostalgia, the Uncanny: The Work of Anna Couani

> The prevailing motif of nostalgia is the closure of the gap between nature and culture, and hence a return to the utopia of biology and symbol united within the walled city of the maternal. (Stewart, 1984:23)

> Somehow the fact that the mother is not phallic means that the mother as mother is lost forever, that the mother as womb, homeland, source and grounding for the subject is irretrievably past. The subject is hence in a foreign land, alienated. (Gallop, 1985:148)

Where does nostalgia begin? And is it not also, precisely, a desire for beginnings, for lost origins? Where then does a subjectivity which refuses the unity of origins situate, or invent, its first moments in memory?

It has been said of ethnic minority writing that it is organised primarily around nostalgia. This is illustrated, for example, in Con Castan's (1986) analysis of Australian Greek writing, which he links with the colonial period and settler writing in Australian literature. Anyone working in this area in Australia will undoubtedly have experienced the repeated and often dismissive response that ethnic minority writing 'simply' deals with nostalgia, and that its mode is elegiac. This usually translates into accusations of a ghetto mentality, or else justifications for the quaint preservation of anachronistic social rituals, ranging from embroidery to marriage customs. The logic appears to be that this writing deals with a landscape of the mind, of memory, which being apparently of minimal relevance to the here and now is therefore something to be outgrown. The US critic Werner Sollors (1986:7–8), in a different context, analyses American ethnic literature in terms of rites of passage, thus reminding all Americans of their codes of initiation and entry. Similarly, the category of ethnic minority writing in this country may be seen, paradoxically, as ultimately feeding the nostalgia of those 'older' white Australians who are reassured that such verifiable codes of cultural difference do indeed exist here. Ethnic minority writing thus returns earlier generations to the scene of their own origins, namely colonial nostalgia.

Within this conceptual framework, the function of nostalgia is to return the unified subject. As explored in Chapter 3, in such a context these writings are relegated to the domain of oral history: the story of a life, the paradigmatic narrative of coherence and closure. Another familiar method of analysing the return of the unified subject through the discourses of nostalgia is to note their supplements, for example the photograph and the souvenir. In his essay on photography, Roland Barthes circles around nostalgia when he writes of the distinction between identity (a matter of legal status) and what he calls the supplement of identity, thus implying the possibility of discovering a core or 'real' self (Barthes, 1984:102). Searching for his dead mother, he discards the many likenesses, and discovers her 'truth', her 'air' (a linking of body and soul), in a childhood photograph which pre-dates his direct memory of her, their shared history (ibid.:107–10). As well as illustrating the unified self, photographs may also signify the return of the dead, the uncanny, the monstrous return of something familiar. And we too will return to the photographic process in relation to Susan Stewart's and Anna Couani's work.

Nostalgia is manifested in its crudest form in the school playground. There the fairy-tales about origins begin—the goose-girl who is really a princess. 'It may appear that I inhabit quite naturally this working-class area on the edge of the city dotted now with more recent migrant tribal outposts but really, at home, my family had, my family were . . . '. The details vary, but the impulse remains the same (Gunew, 1989, 1991). This version comes out of growing up in the 1950s in Melbourne, but it is echoed elsewhere. For example:

> I would not have been capable of writing my poem 'Kaddish' in Australia ten years ago, so uncertain was I of my identification with the Jewish faith and the legitimacy of its existence in a bland Anglo-Saxon context. Nor would I have dared to insert segments of phoneticised Aramaic for fear of revealing that exotic, interloping status of which I was ashamed and afraid . . . Living and growing up in this country has been an exercise in repression. (Zwicky, 1986:91–2)

This represents one particular and poignant tussle with contradictory legitimising narratives. Another émigrée par excellence, Julia Kristeva, reminds us of the 'impossibility of existing without repeated legitimation (without books . . . family)' (Kristeva, 1986:174).

For those who are positioned as individuals in minority groups, these stories indeed offer a kind of legitimation. But what are they for the others, the collective ear, in so far as it exists? There is always a double audience for these stories (Sollors, 1986:7–8). We can speculate, rather crudely, that the impulse to transmit such legitimising narratives arises from a suppression in the public sphere, amounting to the suppression of a particular negotiation of the symbolic order which is often linked with another and prior language.

The term 'symbolic' refers to that Lacanian schema in which the human subject comes into being not so much by acquiring language as through insertion into an already existing order of language and the law: the symbolic order. Such a formulation resists the social dimensions of a specific language, but this does not preclude the consideration entirely (MacCannell, 1986:121–76). Or rather, one needs to ask of the Lacanian scheme exactly why such questions about the particularities of a social order (time, place, language) are precluded. The question raised by this study is that if one sees the symbolic order as constitutive of subjectivity (the possibility of saying 'I' and 'you'), then what occurs to the subject-in-process when it passes from one language system to another? If you like, what it passes through is not *the* mirror-stage but *a* mirror-stage and, what is more, a succession of mirror-stages. Here 'language' means not simply a linguistic system but the varieties of sign systems which constitute a particular cultural domain: behaviour, food, dress, and so on. What kind of subjectivity is created (and what form of suppression takes place) when the subject is forced to enter a new symbolic order? Is it merely suppression or actual repression (the forgetting of what one has forgotten)? What happens to the other and prior language attached to a specific cultural order (Kristeva, 1980:159–209)? Is the first language subsequently rendered alien, shameful, transgressive, particularly if it does not belong to the acceptable repertoire of 'foreign languages'?

In the new order which ethnic minorities enter here in Australia, to what status is their subjectivity (acquired in another order, or, if second-generation, in the context of a particular kind of cultural hybridity) relegated, especially when the father's proper name is forcibly repudiated as illegitimate? This takes place not only in the classic formulations of Lacanian psychoanalysis, where the symbolic order is governed by the name of the father, but also in a cruder thematics, where the loss of the family patronymic (too hard, too foreign) is registered over and over in ethnic minority narratives, often in conjunction with a suppression of the whole language. As Mary Jacobus states in her study of the uncanny in relation to hysteria, 'the death of the father fractures representation and renders living forms unrecognizable' (1986:262). Hence my enquiry into what happens when the subjectivity acquired in one symbolic order is lost in another: are we left with an empty space and a vacated subjectivity? Is it of no significance that the subject enters the symbolic order through a particular language? It would appear that this first subjectivity, by necessity, is suppressed—but where then is its locus? Surely not in the pre-symbolic order which Kristeva, for example, characterises as the domain of the semiotic and the maternal? Does the disowned father become the mother? In the Lacanian scheme it does not make sense to refer to a 'first' symbolic order, but why is this so? Is it possible to speculate, for example, that the subjectivity created in one language is subsequently relocated in the Lacanian Imaginary, where the subject experiences an illusory totality with a phallic mother?

What can be identifed is a process of suppression and the irruption of this suppressed in unpredictable ways—a rhythmic babble, perhaps, for those who inhabit the new cultural order (Kristeva, 1984). Is this how the other languages are heard within Australia? Is the delegitimised name and law of the father reattached to the maternal, the female custodians of these multi-cultures: customs, cooking, costumes and the old tongues, elements in a benignly conceived nostalgia? Derrida, writing of Nietzsche, characterises the mother as that which lives on when the father's name is dead (Derrida, 1985b:16). Indeed, but with what status?

Since my contention here is that the machinery of nostalgia is not simply benign but releases the uncanny, we must again scrutinise the processes of memory and its legitimations. Susan Stewart (1984:145) refers to memory as the mediating link between objects (photographs, souvenirs) and their referents, noting that 'in this gap between resemblance and identity . . . nostalgic desire arises'. Presumably this is a nostalgia for access to direct and unmediated experience, outside a representation which is always either partial or a misrepresentation, and which for the purposes of this chapter will be termed a utopian impulse. Stewart (ibid.:142) traces the process of memory in relation to antiquities, which are seen as public manifestations of the attempt to unfold the origin of a nation and thus to legitimate it as purposeful and unified. Old roots, culture almost merging with nature: isn't it often the way with these quests to imagine or invent a nation? The photograph, that mechanical repetition of identity, may paradoxically serve to undo the concept of the unique and unitary self. Because of this implicit contradiction, Stewart finally locates the authenticity of memory, of a personal history, in the scrapbook which, in its mixed media textures, supposedly defies mechanical reproduction. Composed as it is of multiple fragments, it also incorporates materially the wear and tear of history; and in its collage effects it comprises what we would now term a postmodern artefact. It signifies largely in the private sphere; or, if in the public, as a manifestation and proof of the private. In other words,

most people's scrapbooks—testaments to a private life—are mean-
ingless to others except as arcane inscriptions of the private.

The word 'nostalgia' derives from the Greek: it signifies both 'a
return home' and 'pain', a prolonged absence from home, and
home-sickness. In Freud the closest term to nostalgia is *Heimweh*,
a pregnant term containing the home, the mother, sickness *for*
but also sickness *of* the home. The term also relates to *heimlich*,
secrecy, and *unheimlich*, the uncanny, whose etymology we will
trace in Freud's essay on that theme as a cluster of terms variously
defining a mechanism of repression.

It must be emphasised at this point that psychoanalytic criticism
is not being invoked here as an explanatory device for reading
either the text or (worse) the author as a cluster of symptoms.
More useful is Peter Brooks's contention that literature, like
psychoanalysis, illuminates the structuration or 'dynamic organisation of the psyche'. Brooks traces the interaction of text and
reader in terms of a transferential model which involves 'a real
investment of desire from both sides . . . The transference actual-
izes the past in symbolic form so that it can be repeated, replayed
. . . to a revised version of our stories' (1987:13). For those whose
position *vis-à-vis* these stories is marginal or invisible, the need to
revise them and, above all, the terms in which they are exchanged,
is patently crucial (Chambers, 1985).

The final part of this chapter will attend to the writings of Anna
Couani. Why this choice? Because her work represents one of
those borderline cases which confounds the traditional
commonsense opposition between Australian and migrant or
multicultural writing (neither designation includes British- or
Irish-derived Australians). A further contention throughout this
study is that the term 'migrant' camouflages a hidden distinction
separating Anglo-Celtic and non-Anglo-Celtic writing. Because
Couani is a third-generation Australian writer she can hardly be
classified as 'migrant' in the usual way. But partly because of her
name and the enunciative positions (narrators, implied readers) in
her work, she is often bracketed with the so-called migrant
writers. She is also perceived, and rightly, as an experimental
writer. This poses a problem (as does, for example, the work of
Rosa Cappiello and Ania Walwicz) for those who cordon off

migrant writing as invariably realist on the grounds that the subject simply speaks her/his story, that is, does not write. Such attitudes serve to sustain the fantasy—an imperialist illusion—of what Gayatri Spivak calls the 'native informant': the term indicates an imperialist discursive economy which persists in constructing the colonised subject as unproblematic (Spivak, 1990:59–66). Because of such glaring contradictions and blind spots, in this study (and for reasons discussed in Chapter 1) I use the term 'ethnic minority writing' in preference to earlier alternatives such as migrant writing.

Couani does not simply reproduce those discourses of nostalgia which generally align Europe with civilisation and Anglo-Celtic Australia with the barbarians, and which Ania Walwicz parodies in her poem 'Australia' (in Gunew, 1987a:130). Instead, she contrasts and dislocates the various forms of memory, desire and intimacy at play within them. In Couani's texts, familiar themes in Australian writing function as the terrain of the other (and not of the Lacanian Other[1]) reread, as we shall see, from positions outside. The effect is to liberate the uncanny, and to return the repressed, that secret which lies within the familiar as both a homesickness and sickness of the home. These discourses, juxtaposed in uneasy tension with each other, are grounded by Couani in gender and cultural difference, and a consciously delineated anti-assimilationism. Whether we term this method 'dialogical' (after Bakhtin) or a postmodernist collage which resists closure (Ulmer, 1983), the result is profoundly unsettling for those who subscribe to non-contradictory narratives of nationalism ('the real story'). But, for the present, let us retrace the uncanny in its classic Freudian formulation.

For our purposes the most significant features of Freud's 'The Uncanny' can be found in his statement that it 'is in reality nothing new or alien, but something which is familiar and old-established in the mind and which has become alienated from it only through the process of repression' (Freud, 1976:634). Early in his essay, Freud traces the etymology of the word in various languages beyond the limited equation 'uncanny' = 'unfamiliar'; indeed, his analysis eventually links the home, the family and the secret within both—for secrecy and the uncanny (*heimlich* and *unheimlich*) both contain the word 'home' (*Heim*). The erasure of this distinction embraces many others, such as that between inside and outside, in respect of which Freud cites illustrations of death-in-life, life-in-death. Since the framework of his analysis is Hoffmann's story 'The Sandman', automata (that nineteenth-century obsession) are used to exemplify something dead which appears to live and, conversely, those living who imitate the dead when they indulge in mechanistic behaviour. Here sight becomes the privileged sense and, when threatened, signifies castration. The figure of the double is insurance against death, but also a harbinger of it. Finally, there is the important insight that the main symptom of the uncanny is repetition—the compulsion itself, rather than its content (ibid.:631–2). This is linked in turn to animism and the omnipotence and logic of thought which, like the compulsion to repeat, testifies to the need to control: 'animism, magic and sorcery, the omnipotence of thoughts, man's attitude to death, involuntary repetition and the castration complex com- prise practically all the factors which turn something frightening into something uncanny' (ibid.:632). Subsequent readings of Freud's essay have fallen into the temptation of locating, within the essay itself, an encounter with the uncanny.[2] Freud describes the 'female genital organs' as an '*unheimlich* place . . . the entrance to the former *Heim* [home] of all human beings'. 'When- ever a man dreams of a place or a country', he adds, 'we may interpret the place as being his mother's genitals or her body' (ibid.:637).

The general thesis presented here is that everything we cur- rently term Australian literature (a particular manifestation of the dominant culture) may be reread productively by means of nostal- gia (defined as the liberation of the uncanny) from positions currently outside that literature, as constructed in non-Anglo- Celtic Australian writings. What is then rendered uncanny are precisely the traditional renditions of the home/mother/land for which the referent is arguably an 'Australia' always mediated by somewhere else—the shadow of England, Ireland, and so on. In the writings of those who adopt the cultural positions of Anglo- Celts, 'Australia' is situated paternally, as the father or third term which disrupts the mother–child dyad. 'Australia' is never located in the pre-symbolic, and this is in contrast with a tradition of criticism which has always attempted, as rapidly as possible, to construct an organic link between writing and the land (Gunew, 1990a). 'Australia' is always refracted by particular cultural prisms from elsewhere. In itself this is hardly challenging or new: how could any writing be otherwise than mediated or exist anywhere but in the symbolic order? But what has not been analysed in any detail is the nature of these mediations in relation to a 'home' culture and land. One could argue that the architecture of a collective memory is always bound to a particular place. My suggestion is that the fictions, or meanings, of the allegories we have attached to the old landscape and the old language, as figured in a tradition of writing, have been transposed or transported to this place. Thus 'Australia' exists for us only via these allegories. That the referent for home/mother/land need not inevitably be England or Ireland is the working assumption of this study.

A further question is, what might 'Australia' look like when these other motherlands and languages are acknowledged as constitutive repositories for these allegories? Without these sustaining allegories, these textual legitimations, 'Australia' is the mother who is not the mother, the uncanny place that will *never* give birth: the stillborn. For non-Aboriginal Australians the country is the dead centre, the mother who ingests life (once again we are reminded of Kristevan abjection as discussed in Chapter 3). Life, consequently, is more comfortably located in the cities, on the edge where the land is covered over, pressed under, and where the subject is lost, in the automatic (automaniac) maze: life-in-death, death-in-life. The maternal is always elsewhere, though repressed, in other cultures and languages, though disavowed.

Within 'Australia' the other motherlands irrupt, as described, for example, in Kefala's poem 'The Alien' (1973:20), even when not directly experienced. Certainly, those motherlands are constructed through multiple narrative traditions, notably the various versions of 'England'. Couani's work consistently depicts narrators and implied readers who question and disrupt unexamined assumptions about ordinary 'Australian' life. In her writings there is always the threat of a nameless element which will reposition and rename both the traditional narrative conventions and the subject positions which go with them. In her first collection the shadow of such places is named somewhat arbitrarily 'Italy'—a collection of writings which explore domestic and private alienation. Here the routine and the predictable are in constant danger of being shattered; images abound of sudden accidents to people and to objects. The feeling evoked is that some effort of thought, or prescience, might have averted them; and yet in a way they also seem inevitable, as if such worlds exist to be disrupted. For example, in 'The View' (Couani, 1977:20), the urban landscape is contrasted with the familiar small-town memories of an Australian childhood, exemplified by 'Yesterday and Today' in the same volume:

> What is chronology? It was all the one time in that town . . . Saturday afternoon tennis for the adults, the children roaming bored on the oval. Boredom till it chokes, boredom on the oval, in the car, in the bedroom, in the street and outside the post-office. Sunday boredom in the loungeroom, catching flies in the bay window. (ibid.:15)

Embedded in this recognisable literary territory are slightly disjunctive elements for traditionally positioned 'Anglo/Celtic' readers: for instance, 'Grandpa sang the Internationale, standing, hand on heart' (ibid.:17). And in the last section of this prose poem, where an 'English gent' accosts the adolescent girl narrator, the incident is repeated as though to exorcise it (ibid.:19). There are numerous examples in this volume of typical Anglo-Australian narratives of origins, but here they are situated as other.

In the second collection, *The Train*, 'Xmas in the Bush' is another example of the attempt to atomise and to control, for the latter half of the piece appears to be simply a listing of conversational topics (Couani, 1983:59–61). The form of this listing—as a parodic litany—renders uncanny these otherwise unexceptional topics. The title prose poem in the collection depicts a dreamlike relationship between a man, his family and the other woman/narrator as played out in and around a train 'which is always the past' (ibid.:75–6). The narrator attempts to disentangle the nature of the tragedy haunting the man (is his child blind? his wife?)

before setting fire to the train/the past. In the same volume 'The Detective' depicts a narrator again trying to amass evidence, to understand, but from behind a camera instead of via the distancing surrealism of the previous poem (Couani, 1983:56). The text concludes that 'the evidence is endless', but it leaves hanging the question of the object of this evidence.

Certainly, the impulse to record fragments of scenes and conversations is a dominant organising principle in Couani's work. It evokes the overpowering need to make sense of the ostensibly mundane, and to totally comprehend random experience (as in the persona of the detective); but it also testifies to the impossibility of such an enterprise. The registering of 'evidence' is accompanied by an acute awareness that language itself constitutes a barrier to meaning, particularly in its figurative dimension: 'the fact that a meaning is vague or amorphous, a bit intangible, is not a reason to fabricate a metaphor' (ibid.:49–50). Juxtaposed with these enigmatic attempts to seize and catalogue the mundane, to force it to yield up the secrets belied by its familiar surface, are occasional and often humorous forays into the utopian, as in 'On the Job': 'What would happen if there was a sudden coincidence of social relations with good social relations . . . [?]' (ibid.:55). This quest for the utopian, an alternative model for social organisation, gathers momentum in Couani's later work. In these first two collections this element serves to qualify the narrator both as objective sleuth in the public world and as cynical commentator on intimate relationships in the private domain. With the utopian register, something else enters the fabric of these prose poems.

This imagined perfection warrants further investigation of the trajectory leading from nostalgia to the uncanny. In an interesting attempt to reconnect the Lacanian structure to the social order, Juliet MacCannell describes the unconscious in the following terms:

For Lacan, then, there are two possible versions of the unconscious. The one unconscious, the one of which Freud dreams, is one that we, as speaking, cultured beings have never (yet) experienced. It is the scene of a fictional and retrospective nostalgia for a time and place outside metaphoric enclosures, for language as a neutral 'third term' or common ground that would allow the possibility of the mutual co-recognition of desire between two selves. That which *could have been between* human beings . . . is always prevented . . . by the cultural drive: the drive to organise, to regularise . . . in short, the *basis* of civilisation. (MacCannell, 1984:156–7)

This opposition between anarchic symbiosis and repressive civilisation is a familiar fantasy. On the one hand is a desire for total communication in which language is perceived as transparent; and on the other hand, the cultural order which produces a subjectivity founded on repression. In more general terms, it also echoes Susan Stewart's observation that 'the prevailing motif of nostalgia is the closure of the gap between nature and culture, and hence a return to the utopia of biology and symbol united within the walled city of the maternal' (1984:23).[3] Paradise, as the illusion of a language devoid of the figurative, the nostalgia for utopia, is an element increasingly present in Couani's work, and as we shall see, always encompasses the uncanny.

The sequence of prose poems called *Were All Women Sex-mad?* indicates a new tendency in her work. Much of it is organised in dialogue form, and the interlocutors are sometimes differentiated along gender lines. Whereas in *Italy* and *The Train* the immediate and familiar spaces of the self and domain of the private are framed and analysed by an often objective viewer mimicking a reportage or documentary style (Couani, 1977:33–5), in this sequence of prose poems it is Australia which is depicted as a particular kind of culture, and which is subjected to various interpretations from external (that is, other cultural) vantage points. The private domain (home and family) of the previous volumes is both rejected and nostalgically desired—a sickness for and sickness of the home:

My family comes from 2 different countries and lives in a third country. We gave away the idea of 'home'. No, we laugh at it but we feel the absence of it. We depend on other people, maybe another person, maybe a building, something we own, to give us our sense of home. (Couani, 1982:23)

Chapter 4 ('Remember to Forget') examines in particular the construct 'Australia' from somewhere else. Echoing Wagner's *Tristan and Isolde*, or even Eliot's *The Waste Land*, this chapter begins with an evocation of the fresh salt wind, and the approach to land of two voices in dialogue. Depicted here are the new couple, returning to contemplate the well-known landmass but through a new prism, as a result of incorporating experiences from the old world and of having had to reconstruct 'Australia' there. They project not so much the high romanticism of the doomed couple as a world-weary reappraisal of personal relationships and public spaces:

—Don't go to Australia
—There's no love there
—There is love. It's love which binds us together. But in Australia it's been stretched like a very thin high-tension wire . . . In Australia you can't *want* to love. (Couani, 1982:33)

Australian life, as depicted in two hundred years of officially sanctioned Australian Literature, is here reread and represented 'otherwise'. 'Australia' is a place for a holiday but not to live in, and it is peopled by cynics whose preferred state is silence. It is possible to classify the voices conducting these dialogues as familiar echoes from expatriate narrators and those emanating from the so-called migrant or ethnic ghettos. The clichés erupt in a dialogic sprawl as fragments of conversational analysis which parody the current spate of earnest attempts to fix the national character and ethos. It is not a question of creating a multifarious reality, for 'When you remember something as a visitor it's always typical' (ibid.:31). The voices record the stereotypic and the chapter culminates in a sardonic pillow-talk:

—Afterwards.
—After what?
—After you've felt you weren't loved. When you get used to the idea of not being loved. These secret things take years to understand. I think maybe some people don't ever understand. But now it's changing a bit at last. They're starting to come in from the cold like the old stockman returning to the bright lights

of the station after 2 weeks riding the fences in the cold and the dust. While he's away he has to remember the warmth and light of his home but when he comes back he can forget it.

—He says, And then I get home and wouldn't you know—the wife started her period today. Forget it.

—I think you're starting to understand. (ibid.:33)

Here we encounter in the figure of the stockman the paradigmatic Australian hero-battler, reread from another position than the one informed by nostalgia for the male-dominated nationalist literature of the 1890s.

Running alongside these fragmented conversational collages, like the thread or clue in a detective story, is an apparently unifying device in the shape of a plot concerning an Italian woman who leaves her home in the Australian bush and follows her lover overseas. The family collapses; but whereas the woman is (possibly) raped and then suicides, the former husband finds another woman to replace her. Not only the homeland but, again, the concept of the home (as refuge) is scrutinised:

—She doesn't think that home is something you make, it's something you find . . . she's looking for something she can't quite describe which she'll recognize when she sees . . . It's a migrant problem. (ibid.:36–7)

In brief, the home contains its own conditions for disorder and violence, including the violence of language and particularly the language of love. Both home (through the narrative of the foreign family's demise) and the homeland are undone by something at their core. This sequence of prose poems begins and ends with a country road and a broken home. In the final section presumably the daughter of the dead woman also leaves and escapes to that other arena of desire and possibilities—the city.

Here again we encounter the element of repetition, an overt feature of Couani's work, alongside the impulse to catalogue and classify ('the evidence is endless'). Indeed, the two elements may well be related, as is suggested in Susan Stewart's statement that 'the temporality of everyday life is marked by an irony . . . for this temporality is held to be ongoing and nonreversible and, at the same time, characterized by repetition and predictability' (1984:14).

The gathering of the evidence from everyday life (the unique detail) is incorporated into the contradictory process of repetition and the already known. We are given the minutiae of experience, a moment seized, described in detail, and then re-played, as in 'Untitled', the first prose poem in *Italy*:

> a woman walking down a concrete path towards you and very close, takes off her hat in one sweeping movement of her hand, and takes off her hat in one sweeping movement of her hand, again and again. (Couani, 1977:7)

This repetition, taken from modernist writing and from the cinema, may signify an irruption of the mechanical inside what appears to be life: immediate experience. The seemingly authentic and familiar realism is transmuted into an icon of death-in-life. Moreover, the compulsion to repeat suggests an obsessive desire to read and reread the mundane, to search for clues, in a manner recalling Barthes' pursuit of the truth about his mother. Nothing is revealed, certainly not an authentic observing subject. Images and language collapse: 'And the orange background becomes the blackening arctic sky as the sentence collapses' (ibid.:7). In 'The Never-Dead' the narrator imagines repeated betrayals by her lover; those who have disappeared return over and over again to construct the scene of the uncanny, and to disrupt the traditional unificatory narratives of love.

Whereas the home is the theatre which constantly replays the fragmentation of the subject, the city is occasionally privileged in Couani's work as providing an escape from the constraints of the home, the family, the domestic. The modern city, with its spatial organisation around monuments and centres, has been described by Marc Guillaume (1986:438–9) as an attempt to compensate for the loss of the master narratives of logocentrism (a condition described by Lyotard, 1984). As such master narratives collapse, contemporary city-dwellers seek their own micro-significations, and thus private signs within the public sphere. The city becomes animated and anthropomorphised by this process (Eisenman, 1986:440–1), in which the natural is regularly mourned or nostalgically pursued within the visibly cultural.

Couani's most recent volume, *The Harbour Breathes* (1989),

concentrates on the city as a network of private worlds where the 'evidence' pursued in the earlier volumes has converged with what is now designated a 'secret knowledge'. The volume begins in the following way:

The bridge on the outer quai. The beautiful Sydney has been robbed of its culture as though to pay for beautiful geography. My body's been stripped and wounded and closed up again with plastic parts and metal plates. My heart's gone and the respirator works too hard to oxygenate the atmosphere and the sea spray contains so much detergent that it breaks down my protective layers. I've been torn into and inspected in all my pores and my bowels. Like robot-operated surgery. I wonder why I don't get more angry. Is my city your city, and the city your body like it's my body. Do you feel the lapping of our surf against your side, stroking and soothing your kidneys as the stinking black air pours down your throat, the Pacific for thousands of miles drawing off your wastage. The desert rising like a huge flat mountain beyond the Great Divide and like the natural consequence, the only possible result and closer to what I'm becoming than my love in my city in my body where the cosiness of the buildings bang up against each other and the warm dirty asphalt spreads like a blanket under my feet much more so than grass could. (Couani and Lyssiotis, 1989:1–2)

In the classic structuralist formulation, nature and culture are in an opposite relation to each other; and in the classic move of ideological processes, the cultural artefact (the city) poses as the natural. If the city now incorporates a false culture, what might its opposite be? Within this schema of land and (contained) sea, different subjects project/inhabit different cities. Which is which? Is the self metonymic of the city, or vice-versa? In this first section, both harbour and city are anthropomorphised (remember that Freud relates animism to the imagined omnipotence of thought in the theatre of the uncanny). From the outset, the traditional opposition between nature and culture becomes blurred as 'the warmer dirty asphalt' is more a blanket than grass itself. Here the question of a false culture is raised and recurs throughout the sequence. The body, that implicit seat of the natural, has been refashioned into a cultural artefact and linked with the city's own false culture: it has metamorphosed into Freud's uncanny automaton, the robot, death-in-life. Like the narrator in Eliot's infernal city, the narrator here is suspended ('I'm swinging from a noose') over a pavement which conceals a stream threatening to erupt. This is the archetypal landscape of the uncanny.

In another section of the book, 'Science-Fiction City', the world of the dispossessed, encountered in former works, surfaces once again:

> And I wanted to stay but I had to go. I didn't have a choice. They were leaving and I had to go with them. It all befell me. I wasn't preparing myself for the change. It was a fait accompli. We were going. They already had all their reasons worked out. It was arbitrary and meaningless to me, you know, children. (ibid.:35)

Represented here is yet another succinct evocation of the 'migrant problem', namely the movement from one symbolic order to another, and the concomitant unravelling of identity in cultural dislocation—the fall off the map. Why walk one way rather than another? And when will we return to 'normal'?

This particular work in the sequence begins with the narratorial persona (familiar from other texts) adopting an objective stance and reading, or attempting to read and give meaning to, a character encountered at random. It ends with the disruption of this prosaic activity by death and the uncanny:

> This city loves me. Its changes reflect my moods. The sunset sweeps across the glass walls as I lower my eyes and turn inside for the evening.
>
> He looks up at me before he sleeps. He places a coin on each of his eyes and on the centre of his forehead. He's closed his eyes. (ibid.:37)

Though unremarkable and obvious in the first instance, the phrase 'turn inside for the evening' may be interpreted to include the metamorphosis of the familiar into the monstrously uncanny. The entry into the home can also signify the change inside out, and the final image of self-conscious death (the rituals of death enacted by one who is living) appears to support this reading.

'Parramatta Sestina' deals explicitly with memory and nostalgia:

My memories are my grandma's memories of the city and my mother's talks looking at the mountains, talking about The Ancient, about the beginning of the world like the 2001 movie track but more serious. And Dad feeling alien anywhere west of Parramatta or Broadway even. I felt his sense of relief on the days we came down to the city and he showed me what his Sydney was like.

Where we saw salami and olives in shops I now realize were just like ones in Greece and definitely unlike the big Franklins in the city which sold DEVON (a word my parents pronounced like POISON). There were different city days with Mum, more anglo . . . Just as Mum knew the mountain tracks, Dad knew the city tracks. Not just the steps and pathways around the Cross for example, but he had a mental picture like a map. The shortcuts all the way from the coast to Parramatta. Which makes me think of Sydney as like a middle eastern city, multi-layered and only really knowable by people with that ancient knowledge which is still applicable in the cleaned-up version of Sydney these days. (ibid.:15–16)

The mother is aligned here with the mountains, perhaps with the natural world. The city becomes a palimpsest of micro-narratives—the secret, old and valued knowledge (an echo of the endless quest for evidence in the earlier work). Elsewhere in the sequence, however, the city is described as being filled with the clichés of the already written, as when the narrator states: 'I thought I was there to remember, to notice. But to remember what? The things which occur to me now. Or which occurred to me then' (ibid.:7). This statement economically encompasses the problem of time and space in relation to subjectivity. What kind of subject is created when, and where and how does memory affect the process?

The various images of the city as wasteland (already enumerated) are juxtaposed with—and thus function to qualify—the utopian, conceived of nostalgically as the pre-Oedipal symbiosis, or the Lacanian Imaginary. This is celebrated most directly in 'The Fold', which does not represent the mother so much as the phallic maternal space:

> the fold in the fabric
> the crease on the page
> the lines of your palm
> . . . our history shapes
> in the fold . . . (ibid.: 27)

The fold is the Other conceived as a place of forgotten languages, and as a force which reconciles the apparent split between city and harbour:

> The city is different
> it folds us in
> opens up a space to rest
>
> the harbour breathes us in
> we exhale into the glow of the city lights . . . (ibid.:29)

The mood evoked by this section is contrasted with the fear of separateness and alienation described elsewhere (ibid.:68). In 'The Fold' the narrator's eye and hand create life. Rather than signifying castration, as Freud's essay contends, the eye becomes the condition for life.[4]

It is possible to read the final two prose poems in *The Harbour Breathes* as a further celebration of the utopian as both a good place and no place at all. The potential for other social relations (that other version of the unconscious referred to earlier) is imagined in 'Boundary', where the concerns of much of the earlier work are succinctly conveyed:

> Marking a boundary to define a space. A space to live in. Space for an idea. Marking the boundaries of it. Creating the space, making it empty so something can appear.
>
> Squares of blue sky framed by the window. An object moves across it. A clear shape in the blue.
>
> Clearing a space, marking out a territory. Defining a city. (ibid.:51)

In 'The Pillar of Rooms', the penultimate piece, we are presented with a movement from the dead city to the private world of the couple, a scrap-book of images of a future time converted into a space. The final poem, 'Boundary', takes us from the room of the couple to an empty space which is filled with possibilities rather than evoking the terrors of a totally fragmented identity. The space here is not uncanny because it is indeed *un*familiar, without representing a return of the monstrously familiar. While not necessarily linked to the mother who in earlier collections had been depicted as a 'Polish princess', shades of the goose-princess are evoked as at the beginning of this essay. Space, however, is tenuously connected with the home ('A space to live in') and even with the city, and thus with lived social relations. The pillar of rooms (a temple to change, perhaps) encloses the couple and is transformed into a space where anything might happen. In this case we encounter not cinematic repetitions but cinematic dissolves, the unknown future of the subject:

> Clearing a space, marking out a territory
> Defining a city . . . Throwing time away as though it meant
> nothing. (ibid.:51–2)

In Couani's work the montage derives from a well-known literary terrain, but the voices and scenes are constantly rendered alien and monstrous through being reordered, or viewed from positions somewhere outside, or contrasted with an other and possibly utopian state. Implicit in all her writings is a series of questions. Whose version of Australia is it? What cultural baggage is included in this category? And from whence does it come?

In *The Oxford History of Australian Literature* Leonie Kramer offers the following magisterial pronouncement: 'The diversification of personal histories that one would expect to result from the influx of migrants from many countries of the world has not yet become a marked feature of Australian writing' (Kramer, 1981:8). It would appear that such a colonial machine could indeed be transformed by the explicit inclusion of personal and collective histories from so-called migrants or ethnic minorities. These have existed throughout the last two hundred years and have contributed to the founding narratives of migration as well as offering other constructions of 'Australia'. If they incorporate the element of nostalgia this does not in itself mark them off as a primitive stage in an evolutionary model of a national literature. After all, nostalgia gestures towards the future as well as the past. It may even operate, in culturally specific ways, as a factor in the writings of all those who call themselves Australians, in the forms of sickness for and of an uncanny, monstrously familiar place. Neither race nor place (Stephensen, 1969) ever springs organically from that which in our conscious lives we call home.

Notes

1 Introduction

[1] Official state multiculturalism was set up under Pierre Trudeau to take the heat out of the French–English tensions in Canada (Fleras and Elliott, 1992).

[2] This was revealed to me very clearly in a recent wide-ranging consultancy (Gunew, Papastergiadis and Blonski, 1994a) which we undertook for the Office of Multicultural Affairs concerning the barriers facing NESB writers. It involved looking, among other things, at the whole machinery comprising the publishing, reviewing and teaching of literature in this country. Distinctions were made on the basis of the handy and inept term 'non-English-speaking'; but, surprisingly, Anglo-Celtic interviewees did not differentiate between those born here and those who emigrated here.

[3] The politics of visibility run the risk of reinforcing those metaphors of the visible which reinstate the hegemonic order, as Joan Scott (1991) has pointed out.

[4] For a divergent point of view see Ozolins (1993), who argues that national language policies go beyond and are to some extent in tension with 'ethnically driven' language-maintenance agendas.

2 Marginal Positions

1   The work of the French post-structuralist Michel Foucault has been a considerable influence on Said's text. It is illuminating to look at Said's essays on Foucault (Said, 1984a: chs 9, 10) and an interview in which he discusses his eventual preference for the Black Algerian critic Frantz Fanon (Said, 1986).

2   The study of English as a historical institution complicit with British imperialism has produced many analyses in the last few years. Note in particular J. Batsleer et al., 1988; Eagleton, 1987; Widdowson, 1982; Baldick, 1983; Colls and Dodd, 1986; Hunter, 1988; Doyle, 1989; Bhabha, 1990a.

3   For an overview of African literary theories see Ashcroft, Griffiths and Tiffin, 1989:123–32. See also Chinweizu et al., 1983; Davies and Graves, 1986. For US developments in Black Studies see Gates, Jr, 1984, 1986, 1987, 1988, 1989, 1990, 1992; Smith, 1983; hooks, 1981, 1984, 1989, 1990; Wall, 1989; Willis, 1990. For UK developments in this field see *Feminist Review* 1984; Dabydeen, 1985; Grewal et al., 1988; Hall, 1987, 1988a; Hall et al., 1980; Owusu, 1988. A more recent development has been in the area of Hispanic studies in the US: see Harlow, 1987; Franco, 1989; Anzaldúa, 1990.

3 The Question of Authenticity

1   There is now an avalanche of critiques coming from 'minority' women. For example, Carby, 1982, 1987; Chow, 1991; Collins, 1990; *Feminist Review*, 17; Gates, Jr, 1990; hooks, 1982, 1984; Lorde, 1984; Mohanty et al., 1991; Ogunyemi, 1985; Trinh, 1989. For an attempt by white feminists to respond see Barrett and M. McIntosh, 1985.

2   As Meaghan Morris pointed out when this chapter was first aired as a paper, Lyotard appears to move confusingly between meta- and master-narratives, and in fact we never really escape from either.

3   The concept comes from Dällenbach (1977) and the curious spelling of *abyme* is noted in the introduction.

4   The problem of trying to solve cultural disenfranchisement by

referring to a social justice model is explored in relation to multiculturalism and the arts in Gunew and Rizvi, 1994b.

[5] One notes in passing Jardine's analysis of nostalgia as, in part, centering around critiques of mass culture as 'society without the father' (Jardine, 1985:66–8).

[6] I am referring here to the 'naturalisation process' which migrants must go through in order to become Australian citizens, and also echoing Jardine (1985:24)

4 Antigone Kefala and Ania Walwicz

[1] 'Desire commences as soon as the drives are split off from the subject, consigned forever to a state of non-representation and non-fulfillment. In short, it begins with the subject's emergence into meaning. Desire has its origins not only in the alienation of the subject from its being, but in the subject's perception of its distinctness from the objects with which it earlier identified. It is thus the product of the divisions by means of which the subject is constituted, divisions which inspire in the subject a profound sense of lack. Lacan characterizes desire as "impossible"—impossible both because it derives its energy from the drives, and because it derives its goals from the symbolic' (Silverman, 1983:176).

[2] I am indebted to Judy Brett for alerting me to the prevalence of dreams in Kefala's work. See Brett, 1985:125–33.

[3] The impossibility of coherent subject-formation is also a central problematic in Kristeva's *Powers of Horror* (Kristeva, 1982) where the concept of abjection deals with the inability of the subject to form sustaining boundaries of the self.

5 Rosa Cappiello

[1] In Kristeva's framework it is the phallic mother who regulates the symbolic order: 'As the addressee of every demand, the mother occupies the place of alterity. Her replete body, the receptacle and guarantor of demands, takes the place of all narcissistic, hence imaginary, effects and gratifications; she is,

in other words, the phallus' (Kristeva, 1984:47). An interesting contrast is provided by Mitchell, 1984:297–313.

6 Anna Couani

1. The Lacanian Other (Phallus/God) is the site of truth and the fantasy of attainable satisfaction. The dominant culture poses as this plenitude. In this respect see MacCannell, 1986:61; 166–7.

2. Mary Jacobus (1986) rereads the essay on the uncanny in terms of hysteria. Hélène Cixous (1976) identifies fiction itself as the uncanny, and Janet Todd (1986) locates Freud's own 'blind spot' in the gaze of women.

3. See also Kristeva, 1986:161. Kristeva's emphasis here is less on the idealised archaic mother than on the idealisation of the relationship to her.

4. Janet Todd (1986) argues that in Freud's essay the female gaze has the power to bestow life on the inanimate.

Bibliography

Althusser, L. (1976) *Essays on Ideology*, London: Verso

Anderson, B. (1991) *Imagined Communities: Reflections on the Origin and Spread of Nationalism*, London: Verso

Anderson, P. (1968) 'Components of the National Culture', *New Left Review*, 50, pp. 52–9. Reprinted in A. Cockburn and R. Blackburn (eds) (1969) *Student Power*, Harmondsworth: Penguin, pp. 214–84

Anthias, F. and N. Yuval-Davis (1992) *Racialized Boundaries: Race, Nation, Gender, Colour and the Anti-racist Struggle*, London: Routledge

Anzaldúa, G. (ed.) (1990) *Making Face, Making Soul (Haciendo Caras): Creative and Critical Perspectives by Women of Color*, San Francisco: Aunt Lute

Ariès, P. (1979) *Centuries of Childhood*, Harmondsworth: Penguin

Ashcroft, B., G. Griffiths and H. Tiffin (1989) *The Empire Writes Back: Theory and Practice in Post-Colonial Literatures*, London: Routledge

Bakhtin, M. (1968) *Rabelais and His World,* Cambridge and Massachusetts: MIT Press

—— (1984) *Problems of Dostoievsky's Poetics*, Minneapolis: University of Minnesota Press

Baldick, C. (1983) *The Social Mission of English Criticism 1848–1932*, Oxford: Clarendon Press

Barrett, M. and M. McIntosh (1985) 'Ethnocentrism and Socialist Feminist Theory', *Feminist Review*, 20, Summer, pp. 23–47

Barthes, R. (1967) *Writing Degree Zero*, trans. A. Lavers and C. Smith, London: Cape

—— (1975) *The Pleasure of the Text*, trans. R. Miller, New York: Hill & Wang

—— (1984) *Camera Lucida*, trans. R. Miller, London: Fontana

Batsleer, J. et al. (1985) *Re-writing English*, London: Methuen

Belsey, C. (1985) *The Subject of Tragedy: Identity and Difference in Renaissance Drama*, London: Methuen

Bennett, T. (1992a) 'Putting Policy into Cultural Studies', in L. Grossberg, C. Nelson and P. Treichler (eds), *Cultural Studies*, New York: Routledge, pp. 23–37

—— (1992b) 'Coming Out of English: A Policy Calculus for Cultural Studies' in K. K. Ruthven (ed.), *Beyond the Disciplines: The New Humanities*, Canberra: Australian Academy of the Humanities, pp. 33–44

Benterrak, K., S. Muecke and P. Roe (1984) *Reading the Country*, Fremantle: Fremantle Arts Centre Press

Bhabha, H. K. (1983a) 'Difference, Discrimination and the Discourse of Colonialism', in F. Barker et al. (eds), *The Politics of Theory*, Colchester: University of Sussex, pp. 194–211

—— (1983b) 'The Other Question—the Stereotype and Colonial Discourse', *Screen*, 24, 6, November–December, pp. 18–36

—— (1984a) 'Representation and the Colonial Text: A Critical Exploration of Some Forms of Mimeticism', in F. Gloversmith (ed.), *The Theory of Reading*, Sussex: Harvester, pp. 93–122

—— (1984b) 'Of Mimicry and Man: The Ambivalence of Colonial Discourse', *October*, 28, pp. 125–33

—— (1985a) 'Signs Taken for Wonders: Questions of Ambivalence and Authority Under a Tree Outside Delhi, May 1817', in F. Barker et al. (eds), *Europe and Its Others*, vol. 1, Colchester: University of Essex, pp. 89–106. Also in H. L. Gates Jr (ed.) (1986) *'Race', Writing and Difference*, Chicago: University of Chicago Press, pp. 163–84

—— (1985b) 'Sly Civility', October, 34, pp. 71–80

—— (1988) 'The Commitment to Theory', *New Formations*, 5, pp. 5–23

—— (ed.) (1990a) *Nation and Narration*, London: Routledge

—— (1990b) 'Introduction' and 'DissemiNation' in H. Bhabha (ed.), *Nation and Narration*, London: Routledge, pp. 1–7; 291–322

—— (1990c) 'Interrogating Identity: The Postcolonial Prerogative', in D. T. Goldberg (ed.), *Anatomy of Racism*, Minneapolis: University of Minnesota Press, pp. 183–209

—— (1990d) 'Interview: The Third Space', in J. Rutherford (ed.), *Identity: Community, Culture, Difference*, London: Lawrence & Wishart, pp. 207–22

—— (1991) 'The Postcolonial Critic—Homi Bhabha Interviewed by David Bennett and Terry Collits', *Arena*, 96, pp. 47–63

—— (1994) *The Location of Culture*, London: Routledge

Blonski, A. (1992) *Arts for a Multicultural Australia 1973–1991. An Account of Australia Council Policies*, Sydney: Australia Council

—— (ed.) (1993) 'Australian Film and Video Issue', *Artlink*, 13, 1, March–May

Boelhower, W. (1987) *Through a Glass Darkly: Ethnic Semiosis in American Literature*, New York: Oxford University Press

Brennan, T. (1989) *Salman Rushdie and the Third World: Myths of the Nation*, New York: St Martin's Press

Brett, J. (1985) 'The Process of Becoming: Antigone Kefala's *The First Journey* and *The Island*', *Meanjin*, 44, 1, March, pp. 125–33

Brooks, P. (1987) 'The Idea of a Psychoanalytic Literary Criticism', in S. Rimmon-Kenan (ed.), *Discourse in Psychoanalysis and Literature,* London: Methuen, pp. 1–18

Burniston, S. and C. Weedon (1978) 'Ideology, Subjectivity and the Artistic Text', in Centre for Contemporary Cultural Studies, *On Ideology*, London: Hutchinson, pp. 199–229

Cappiello, R. (1981) *Paese Fortunato*, Milan: Feltrinelli

—— (1984) *Oh Lucky Country*, trans. G. Rando, Brisbane: University of Queensland Press

—— (1987) 'Why I Write What I Write', *Australian Society*, January, pp. 25–6

Carby, H. (1982) 'White Woman Listen! Black Feminism and the Boundaries of Sisterhood', in Centre for Contemporary Cultural Studies, *The Empire Strikes Back*, London: Hutchinson, pp. 212–35

—— (1987) *Reconstructing Womanhood: The Emergence of the Afro-American Woman Novelist*, New York: Oxford University Press

Carter, P. (1992) *Living in a New Country*, London: Faber

Castan, C. (1986) 'Ethnic Australian Writing. Is it Really Australian Literature?', *Outrider*, 3, 2, December, pp. 64–79

Castles, S. et al. (1988) 'The Bicentenary and the Failure of Australian Nationalism', *Race and Class*, 29, 3, pp. 53–68

Chambers, R. (1985) *Story and Situation: Narrative Seduction and the Power of Fiction*, Minneapolis: University of Minnesota Press

Chinweizu et al. (1983) *Toward the Decolonization of African Literature*, vol. 1, Washington: Howard University Press

Chow, R. (1991) *Women and Chinese Modernity: The Politics of Reading Between East and West*, Minnapolis: University of Minnesota Press

Cixous, H. (1976) 'Fiction and its Phantoms: A Reading of Freud's Das Unheimliche (The "uncanny")', *New Literary History*, 7, 3, Spring, pp. 525–48

Clifford, J. et al. (1987) 'Of Other Peoples: Beyond the "Salvage" Paradigm', in H. Foster (ed.), *Discussions in Contemporary Culture*, DIA Art Foundation 1, Seattle: Bay Press, pp. 122–5

—— (1989) 'Notes on Theory and Travel', *Inscriptions*, 5, pp. 177–88

Clyne, M. (1991) *Community Languages: The Australian Experience*, Melbourne: Cambridge University Press

Collins, P. H. (1990) *Black Feminist Thought: Knowledge, Consciousness and the Politics of Empowerment*, New York: Routledge

Colls, R. and P. Dodd (eds) (1986) *Englishness: Politics and Culture 1880–1920*, London: Croom Helm

Couani, A. (1977) *Italy*, Melbourne: Rigmarole

—— (1982) *Were All Women Sex-mad?*, Melbourne: Rigmarole

—— (1983) *The Train*, in B. Brooks and A. Couani, *Leaving Queensland and The Train*, Sydney: Sea Cruise Books

—— and Gunew, S. (eds) (1988) *Telling Ways: Australian Wom-*

en's Experimental Writing, Adelaide: Australian Feminist Studies

—— and P. Lyssiotis (1989) *The Harbour Breathes*, Sydney and Melbourne: Masterthief Enterprises and Sea Cruise Books

Creed, B. (1986) 'Horror and the Monstrous-Feminine: An Imaginary Abjection', *Screen*, 27, 1, pp. 44–70

Cunningham, S. (1992) *Framing Culture: Criticism and Policy in Australia*, Sydney: Allen & Unwin

Dabydeen, D. (ed.) (1985) *The Black Presence in English Literature*, Manchester: Manchester University Press

Dällenbach, L. (1977) *Le Récit Spéculaire. Essai sur le mise en abyme*, Paris: Éditions du Seuil

Dante (1962) *Inferno*, trans. T. Okey, London: J. M. Dent

Davies, C. B. and A. A. Graves (eds) (1986) *Ngambika: Studies of Women in African Literature*, New Jersey: Africa World Press

Davis, J. and B. Hodge (eds) (1985) *Aboriginal Writing Today*, Canberra: Australian Institute of Aboriginal Studies

Davis, N. Z. (1978) 'Women On Top: Symbolic Sexual Inversion and Political Disorder in Early Modern Europe', in B. A. Babcock (ed.), *The Reversible World*, Ithaca: Cornell University Press, pp. 147–89

Davison, D. (1992) 'Knocked by a Heady Bouquet', *Australian*, September, pp. 5–6

de Lauretis, T. (1984) *Alice Doesn't: Feminism, Semiotics, Cinema*, London: Macmillan

de Man, P. (1985) '"Conclusions" on Walter Benjamin's "The Task of the Translator"', *Yale French Studies*, 69, pp. 25–46

Deleuze, G. and F. Guattari (1986) *Kafka: Toward a Minor Literature*, Minneapolis: University of Minnesota Press

Delphy, C. (1984) *Close to Home: A Materialist Analysis of Women's Oppression*, London: Hutchinson

Derrida, J. (1969) 'The Ends of Man', *Philosophy and Phenomenological Research*, 30, September, pp. 31–57

—— (1974) *Of Grammatology*, trans. G. C. Spivak, Baltimore: Johns Hopkins University Press

—— (1979) 'The Parergon', *October*, 9, pp. 3–40

—— (1985a) 'Des Tours de Babel', in J. F. Graham (ed.), *Differ-*

ence in Translation, Ithaca: Cornell University Press, pp. 165–248

—— (1985b) *The Ear of the Other*, ed. C. V. McDonald, New York: Schocken Books

Doyle, B. (1989) *English and Englishness*, London: Routledge

Dutton, G. (1978) 'Why Our Oldies Are So Good', *Bulletin*, 25 July, p. 62

Dyer, R. (1988) 'White', *Screen*, 29, 4, Autumn, pp. 44–64

Eagleton, T. (1983) *Literary Theory: An Introduction*, Oxford: Blackwell.

—— (1984) *The Function of Criticism*, London: Verso

—— (1987) 'The End of English', *Textual Practice*, Spring, pp. 1–9

—— (1991) *Ideology: An Introduction*, London: Verso

Eco, U. (1984) *Reflections on 'The Name of the Rose'*, London: Secker & Warburg

Eisenman, P. (1986) 'The City as Memory and Immanence', in M. Feher and S. Kwinter (eds), *Zone*, 1/2, New York: Urzone Inc., pp. 440–1

Ellmann, M. (1979) *Thinking About Women*, London: Virago

Feminist Review, 1984, vol. 17, Autumn (whole issue on Black women's writing)

Ferrier, C. (ed.) (1985) *Gender, Politics and Fiction*, Brisbane: University of Queensland Press

Fischer, M. (1986) 'Ethnicity and the Post-Modern Arts of Memory', in J. Clifford et al. (eds), *Writing Culture: The Poetics and Politics of Ethnography*, Berkeley: University of California Press, pp. 194–233

Fleras, A. and J. L. Elliott (1992) *Multiculturalism in Canada: The Challenge of Diversity*, Scarborough: Nelson Canada

Foucault, M. (1979) *Michel Foucault: Power, Truth, Strategy*, ed. M. Morris and P. Patton, Sydney: Feral Publications

—— (1980) *Power/Knowledge: Selected Interviews and Other Writings 1972–1977*, ed. G. Gordon, New York: Pantheon Books

Franco, J. (1989) *Plotting Women: Gender and Representation in Mexico*, Verso: London

Freadman, A. (1985) 'Taking Things Literally (Sins of My Old Age)', *Southern Review*, 18, 2, July, pp. 161–88

Freud, S. (1976) 'The Uncanny', *New Literary History*, 7, 3, Spring, pp. 619–45

Gallop, J. (1985) *Reading Lacan*, Ithaca: Cornell University Press

Gatens, M. (1990) 'A Critique of the Sex/Gender Distinction', in S. Gunew (ed.), *A Reader in Feminist Knowledge*, London: Routledge, 139–57

Gates, H. L. Jr (ed.) (1984) *Black Literature and Literary Theory*, New York: Methuen

—— (ed.) (1986) *'Race', Writing and Difference*, Chicago: University of Chicago Press

—— (1987) 'Authority, (White) Power and the (Black) Critic: Or, It's All Greek to Me', *Cultural Critique*, 7, Fall, pp. 19–46

—— (1988) *The Signifying Monkey: A Theory of African-American Literary Criticism*, New York: Oxford University Press

—— (1989) *Figures in Black: Words, Signs, and the 'Racial' Self*, New York: Oxford University Press

—— ed. (1990) *Reading Black, Reading Feminist: A Critical Anthology*, New York: Meridian

—— (1992) *Loose Canons: Notes on the Culture Wars*, New York: Oxford University Press

Geertz, C. (1973) *The Interpretation of Cultures: Selected Essays*, New York: Basic Books

Gibbs, A. (1989–90) 'These Are Notes: Ania Walwicz's Writing', *Age Monthly Review*, 9, 9, December, pp. 9–10

Gillett, S. (1991) 'At the Beginning: Ania Walwicz's Writing', *Southerly*, 2, pp. 239–52

Grewal, S. et al. (1988) *Charting the Journey: Writings by Black and Third World Women*, London: Sheba

Grosz, E. (1989) *Sexual Subversions: Three French Feminists*, Sydney: Allen & Unwin

—— (1990) 'Contemporary Theories of Power and Subjectivity' in S. Gunew (ed.), *Feminist Knowledge: Critique and Construct*, London: Routledge, pp. 59–120

—— (1994) *Volatile Bodies. Towards a Corporeal Feminism*, Bloomington: Indiana University Press

Guillaume, M. (1986) 'Questionnaire' in M. Feher and S. Kwinter (eds), *Zone*, 1/2, New York: Urzone Inc., pp. 438–9

Gunew, S. (ed.) (1981) *Displacements: Migrant Storytellers*, Geelong, Vic.: Deakin University Press

—— (1985) 'Migrant Women Writers: Who's on Whose Margins?' in C. Ferrier (ed.), *Gender, Politics and Fiction*, Brisbane: University of Queensland Press, pp. 163–78

—— (ed.) (1987a) *Displacements 2; Multicultural Storytellers*, Geelong, Vic.: Deakin University Press

—— (1987b) 'Culture, Gender and the Author-Function: Wongar's *Walg*', *Southern Review*, 20, 3, pp. 261–70

—— (1989) 'Memory Crop', in D. Modjeska (ed.), *Inner Cities*, Ringwood: Penguin, pp. 219–28

—— (1990a) 'Denaturalizing Cultural Nationalisms: Multicultural Readings of Australia', in H. Bhabha (ed.), *Nation and Narration*, London: Routledge, pp. 99–120

—— (1990b) 'Feminist Knowledge: Critique and Construct', in S. Gunew (ed.), *Feminist Knowledge: Critique and Construct*, London: Routledge, pp. 13–35

—— (1991) 'Bulgaria: Personal History of an Unknown Country', in G. Papaellinas (ed.), *Homeland*, Sydney: Allen & Unwin, pp. 83–92

—— (ed.) (1992) *Typereader 7*, Geelong, Vic.: Centre for Studies in Literary Education, Deakin University

—— (1993a) 'Multicultural Multiplicities: Canada, USA, Australia', *Meanjin*, 52, 3, September, pp. 447–61

—— (1993b) 'Against Multiculturalism: Rhetorical Images', in G. L. Clark, D. Forbes and R. Francis (eds), *Multiculturalism, Difference and Postmodernism*, Melbourne: Longman Cheshire, pp. 38–53

—— (1993c) 'Feminism and the Politics of Irreducible Differences: Multiculturalism/Ethnicity/Race', in S. Gunew and A. Yeatman (eds), *Feminism and the Politics of Difference*, Sydney: Allen & Unwin, pp. 1–19

—— and J. Mahyuddin (eds) (1988) *Beyond the Echo: Multicultural Women's Writing*, Brisbane: Queensland University Press

——, L. Houbein, A. Karakostas-Seda and J. Mahyuddin (eds) (1992a) *A Bibliography of Australian Multicultural Writers*, Geelong, Vic.: Centre for Studies in Literary Education, Deakin University

—— and K. O. Longley (eds) (1992b) *Striking Chords: Multicultural Literary Criticism*, Sydney: Allen & Unwin

—— and A. Yeatman (eds) (1993) *Feminism and the Politics of Difference*, Sydney: Allen & Unwin

——, N. Papastergiadis and A. Blonski (1994a) *Access to Excellence: A Review of Issues Affecting Artists and Arts from Non-English Speaking Backgrounds*, vol. 2, *Writers*, commissioned by the Office of Multicultural Affairs, Canberra: Australian Government Publishing Service

—— and F. Rizvi (eds) (1994b) *Culture, Difference and the Arts*, Sydney: Allen & Unwin

Hall, S. (1987) 'Minimal Selves', in L. Appignanesi (ed.), *Identity*, ICA Documents, 6, London: ICA, pp. 44–6

—— (1988a) 'New Ethnicities', in K. Mercer (ed.), *Black Film British Cinema*, London: Institute of Contemporary Arts, pp. 27–30

—— (1988b) 'Thatcher's Lessons', *Marxism Today*, March, p. 23

—— (1988c) 'Brave New World', *Marxism Today*, October, p. 24

—— (1989) 'Cultural Identity and Cinematic Representation', *Framework*, 36, pp. 68–81

—— (1990) 'Cultural Identity and Diaspora', in J. Rutherford (ed.), *Identity: Community, Culture, Difference*, London: Lawrence & Wishart, pp. 222–37

—— et al. (eds) (1980) *Culture Media Language*, London: Hutchinson

Haraway, D. (1989) *Primate Visions: Gender, Race, and Nature in the World of Modern Science*, New York: Routledge

—— (1991) *Simians, Cyborgs and Women: The Reinvention of Nature*, London: Free Association Books

Harlow, B. (1987) *Resistance Literature*, New York: Methuen

—— (1989) 'Commentary: "All That is Inside is not Center": Responses to the Discourses of Domination', in E. Weed (ed.) *Coming To Terms: Feminism, Theory, Politics*, New York: Routledge, pp. 162–70

Hartman, G. (1980) *Criticism in the Wilderness*, New Haven: Yale University Press

Hartsock, N. (1987) 'Rethinking Modernism: Minority vs. Majority Theories', *Cultural Critique*, 7, Fall, pp. 187–206

Hatzimanolis, E. (1990) 'The Politics of Nostalgia: Community and

Difference in Migrant Writing', *Hecate*, 16, 1/2, pp. 120–7

Henriques, J. (1984) 'Social Psychology and the Politics of Racism', in *Changing the Subject: Psychology, Social Regulation and Subjectivity*, London: Methuen, pp. 60–89

Hirst, P. (1979) *On Law and Ideology*, London: Macmillan

Hobsbawm, E. and T. Ranger (eds) (1983) *The Invention of Tradition*, Cambridge: Cambridge University Press

hooks, bell (1982) *Ain't I a Woman*, London: Pluto Press

—— (1984) *Feminist Theory: From Margin to Center*, Boston: South End Press

—— (1989) *Talking Back: Thinking Feminist, Thinking Black*, Boston: South End Press

—— (1990) *Yearning: Race, Gender, and Cultural Politics*, Boston: South End Press

Hunter, I. (1988) *Culture and Government: The Emergence of Literary Education*, London: Macmillan

Hunter, I., D. Meredyth, B. Smith and G. Stokes (1991) *Accounting for the Humanities*, Brisbane: Institute for Cultural Policy Studies

Hutcheon, L. (1991) *Splitting Images: Contemporary Canadian Ironies*, Toronto: Oxford University Press

—— and M. Richmond (eds) (1990) *Other Solitudes: Canadian Multicultural Fictions*, Toronto: Oxford University Press

Jacobson, L. (1990) 'Reading Ania Walwicz', *Outrider*, 90, pp. 148–59

Jacobus, M. (1986) *Reading Women: Essays in Feminist Criticism*, New York: Columbia University Press

JanMohammed, A. and D. Lloyd (1987) 'Introduction: Minority Discourse—What is to be Done?' *Cultural Critique*, 7, Fall, pp. 5–18

Jardine, A. (1985) *Gynesis: Configurations of Woman and Modernity*, Ithaca and London: Cornell University Press

Julien, I. and K. Mercer (1988) 'Introduction—De Margin and De Centre', *Screen*, 29, 4, Autumn, pp. 2–11

Junius, (1976) 'Balkan Light', *24 Hours*, March, p. 48

Jupp, J. (ed.) (1988) *The Australian People: An Encyclopedia of the Nation, Its People and Their Origins*, Sydney: Angus & Robertson

Kamuf, P. (1988) *Signature Pieces: On the Institution of Author-ship*, Ithaca: Cornell University Press

Kaplan, C. (1987) 'Deterritorializations: The Rewriting of Home and Exile in Western Feminist Discourse', *Cultural Critique*, 6, Spring, pp. 187–98

Kee, Poo-Kong (1986) *Conceptualising and Measuring Ethnic Origin and Identification: the Australian, Canadian, American and British Experience*, Melbourne: Australian Institute of Multicultural Affairs (Occasional Paper No.5)

Kefala, A. (1973) *The Alien*, Brisbane: Makar

—— (1975) *The First Journey: Two Short Novels*, Sydney: Wild & Woolley

—— (1978) *Thirsty Weather*, Victoria: Outback Press

—— (1984a) *The Island*, Sydney: Hale & Iremonger

—— (1984b) *Alexia*, Sydney: John Ferguson

—— (1988a) *European Notebook*, Sydney: Hale & Iremonger

—— (1988b) 'Towards a Language', in K. H. Petersen and A. Rutherford (eds), *Displaced Persons*, Denmark: Dangaroo Press, pp. 75–82

—— (1992) *Absence: New and Selected Poems*, Sydney: Hale & Iremonger

Kim, D. (1976) 'The Mood is Loneliness', *Sydney Morning Herald*, 26 June

Kramer, L. (1981) 'Introduction' in *The Oxford History of Australian Literature*, Melbourne: Oxford University Press, pp. 1–23

Kristeva, J. (1980) *Desire in Language*, Oxford: Blackwell

—— (1982) *Powers of Horror: an Essay on Abjection*, trans. L. Roudiez, New York: Columbia University Press

—— (1984) *Revolution in Poetic Language*, New York: Columbia University Press

—— (1986) *The Kristeva Reader*, ed. T. Moi, New York: Columbia University Press

Lacan, J. (1977a) *The Four Fundamental Concepts of Psycho-analysis*, Harmondsworth: Penguin

—— (1977b) *Ecrits*, London: Tavistock

Lewitt, M. (1980) *Come Spring*, Melbourne: Scribe

—— (1985) *No Snow in December*, Melbourne: Heinemann

Lindsay, E. (1979) 'Two Poets: Different Visions', *24 Hours*, January, p. 65

Lloyd, D. (1987) 'Genet's Genealogy: European Minorities and the Ends of the Canon', *Cultural Critique*, 6, Spring, pp. 161–86

Lloyd, G. (1984) *The Man of Reason*, London: Methuen

Lorde, A. (1984) *Sister Outsider*, New York: The Crossing Press

Loriggio, F. (1990a) 'History, Literary History, and Ethnic Literature', in J. Pivato (ed.) *Literatures of Lesser Diffusion*, Alberta: Research Institute for Comparative Literature, pp. 21–45

—— (1990b) 'Italian-Canadian Literature: Basic Critical Issues', in D. Minni and A. F. Campolini (eds), *Writers in Transition*, Montréal: Guernica, pp. 73–96

Lyotard, J.-F. (1984) *The Post-modern Condition: A Report on Knowledge*, Manchester: Manchester University Press

—— (1986) 'Defining the Postmodern', in L. Appignanesi (ed.), *Postmodernism*, London: Institute for Contemporary Art, pp. 6–7

—— (1989) 'Universal History and Cultural Difference', in Andrew Benjamin (ed.), *The Lyotard Reader*, Oxford: Blackwell, pp. 314–23

MacCannell, J. F. (1986) *Figuring Lacan: Criticism and the Cultural Unconscious*, Lincoln: University of Nebraska Press

Macklin, R. (1985) 'Coping with the Lucky Country', *Australian*, 12 January

Malouf, D. (1985) 'Interview', *Outrider*, 2, 2, December, pp. 59–71

Mani, L. (1985) 'The Production of an Official Discourse on *Sati* in Early Nineteenth-Century Bengal', in F. Barker et al. (eds), *Europe and Its Others*, vol. 1, Colchester: University of Essex, pp. 107–27

Markale, J. (1975) *Women of the Celts*, trans. A. Mygind, C. Hauch and P. Henry, London: Gordon Cremonesi

Mercier, V. (1969) *The Irish Comic Tradition*, London: Oxford University Press

Milner, A. (1985) 'The "English" Ideology: Literary Criticism in England and Australia', *Thesis XI*, 12, pp. 110–29

Mitchell, J. (1984) *Women: the Longest Revolution*, London: Virago

Modjeska, D. (1981) *Exiles At Home*, Sydney: Sirius

Mohanty, C. (1988) 'Under Western Eyes: Feminist Scholarship and Colonial Discourses', *Feminist Review*, 30, Autumn, pp. 61–86

——— et al. (eds) (1991) *Third World Women and the Politics of Feminism*, Bloomington: Indiana University Press

Moi, T. (1985) *Sexual/Textual Politics*, London: Methuen

Nairn, T. (1977) *The Break-up of Britain: Crisis and Neo-Nationalism*, London: NLB

Norris, C. (1982) *Deconstruction: Theory and Practice*, London: Methuen

Oakley, B. (1992) 'In the First Place', *Australian Magazine*, 20–21 June, p. 8

Office of Multicultural Affairs (1989) *National Agenda for A Multicultural Australia*, Canberra: Australian Government Publishing Service

Ogunyemi, C. O. (1985) 'Womanism: The Dynamics of the Contemporary Black Female Novel in English', *Signs*, 11, 1 Autumn, pp. 63–80

Olivier, C. (1989) *Jocasta's Children: The Imprint of the Mother*, trans. G. Craig, London: Routledge

Outlaw, L. (1990) 'Toward a Critical Theory of "Race"', in D. T. Goldberg (ed.), *Anatomy of Racism*, Minneapolis: University of Minnesota Press, pp. 58–82

Owen, C. (1985) 'Posing', in *Difference: On Representation and Sexuality*, New York: The New Museum of Contemporary Art, pp. 7–18

Owusu, K. (ed.) (1988) *Storms of the Heart: An Anthology of Black Arts and Culture*, London: Camden Press

Ozolins, Uldis (1993) *The Politics of Language in Australia*, Melbourne: Cambridge University Press

Padolsky, E. (1991) 'Cultural Diversity and Canadian Literature: A Pluralist Approach to Majority and Minority Writing in Canada', *International Journal of Canadian Studies*, 3, Spring, pp. 111–28

——— (1992) 'Establishing the Two-Way Street: Literary Criticism and Ethnic Studies', *Canadian Ethnic Studies*, 22, 1, pp. 22–37

Page, G. (1989) 'An Unorthodox Biography', *Canberra Times*, 12 February

Papastergiadis, N. (1992) 'The Journeys Within: Migrant and Identity in Greek-Australian Literature', in S. Gunew and K. O. Longley (eds), *Striking Chords: Multicultural Literary Inter-*

pretations, Sydney: Allen & Unwin, pp. 149–61

—— (1993) *Modernity as Exile: The Stranger in John Berger's Writing*, Manchester: Manchester University Press

Parry, B. (1987) 'Problems in Current Theories of Colonial Discourse', *Oxford Literary Review*, 9, 1–2, pp. 27–58

Pearson, D. (1991) 'Biculturalism and Multiculturalism in Comparative Perspective', in P. Spoonley, D. Pearson and C. Macpherson (eds), *Nga Take: Ethnic Relations and Racism in Aotearoa/New Zealand*, North Palmerston, New Zealand: Dunmore Press, pp. 194–214

Pivato, J. (1994) *Echo: Essays on Other Literatures*, Montréal: Guernica Editions

Π. O. (ed.) (1985) *Off the Record*, Ringwood: Penguin Books

Porter, D. (1983) 'Orientalism and its Problems', in F. Barker et al. (eds), *The Politics of Theory*, Colchester: University of Sussex, pp. 179–93

Rando, G. (1984) 'Introduction', in R. Cappiello, *Oh Lucky Country*, Brisbane: University of Queensland Press, pp. v–xi

Rich, A. (1986) 'Notes Toward a Politics of Location (1984)', in *Blood, Bread and Poetry: Selected Prose 1979–1985*, London: Virago, pp. 210–31

Rizvi, F. (1989) *Multiculturalism: Making Policy for a Polyethnic Society*, vol. C of *Migration, Ethnicity and Multiculturalism* (SSS 318), Geelong, Vic.: Deakin University Press

—— (forthcoming) *Australian Racism*, Melbourne: Oxford University Press

Rizzo, S. (1992) 'Interview with Rosa Cappiello', *New Literatures Review*, 24, pp. 117–22

Rothfield, P. (1990) 'Feminism, Subjectivity, and Sexual Difference', in S. Gunew (ed.), *Feminist Knowledge: Critique and Construct*, London: Routledge, pp. 121–44

Rushdie, S. (1991) *Imaginary Homelands*, London: Granta

Said, E. (1979) *Orientalism*, New York: Vintage Books

—— (1983) 'Opponents, Audiences, Constituencies and Community', in H. Foster (ed.), *Postmodern Culture*, London: Pluto Press, pp. 135–59

—— (1984a) *The World, The Text, and the Critic*, London: Faber

—— (1984b) 'Reflections on Exile', in *Granta*, 13, UK, pp. 157–72

—— (1985) 'Orientalism Reconsidered', in F. Barker et al. (eds),

Europe and Its Others, vol. 1, Colchester: University of Essex, pp. 14–27

—— (1986) 'Interview', G. Hentzi and A. McClintock, *Critical Texts. A Review of Theory and Criticism*, 3, 2, Winter, pp. 6–13

—— (1987) 'Interview', in Imre Saluzinsky, *Criticism in Society*, New York: Methuen, pp. 122–48

—— (1989) 'Representing the Colonized: Anthropology's Interlocutors', *Critical Inquiry*, 15, 2, Winter, pp. 205–25

—— (1990) 'In the Shadow of the West: An Interview with Edward Said' with P. Mariani and J. Crary, in R. Ferguson et al. (eds) *Discourses: Conversations in Postmodern Art and Culture*, Cambridge, Mass.: New Museum of Contemporary Art, MIT Press, pp. 93–103

—— (1993) *Culture and Imperialism*, London: Chatto & Windus

Sangari, K. K. (1987) 'The Politics of the Possible', *Cultural Critique*, 7, Fall, pp. 157–86

Schaffer, K. (1988) *Women and the Bush: Forces of Desire in the Australian Cultural Tradition*, Sydney: Cambridge University Press

Schiavoni, F. (1982) 'Terror Australiana: A Cry from the Ghetto', *Age Monthly Review*, 2, 6, October, pp. 8–9

Schor, N. (1985) *Breaking the Chain: Women, Theory and French Realist Fiction*, New York: Columbia University Press

Scott, J. W. (1991) 'The Evidence of Experience', *Critical Inquiry*, 17, Summer, pp. 773–97

Shapcott, T. (1973) 'Australian Poetry: Now is Then', *Australian Book Review*, 73

Silverman, K. (1983) *The Subject of Semiotics*, New York: Oxford University Press

Sivaramakrishnan, A. (1989) 'The Slave With Two Hearts: The Asymmetry of Cultural Assimilation', *Third Text*, 7, Summer, pp. 3–10

Smith, B. (ed.) (1983) *Home Girls: A Black Feminist Anthology*, New York: Kitchen Table Women of Color Press

Sollors, W. (1986) *Beyond Ethnicity: Consent and Descent in American Culture*, New York: Oxford University Press

—— (ed.) (1989) *The Invention of Ethnicity*, New York: Oxford University Press

Spivak, G. (1983) 'Displacement and the Discourse of Woman', in M. Krupnick (ed.), *Displacement: Derrida and After*, Bloomington: Indiana University Press, pp. 169–95

—— (1985) 'The Rani of Simur', in F. Barker et al. (eds), *Europe and Its Others*, vol. 1, Colchester: University of Essex, pp. 128–51

—— (1986) 'Imperialism and Sexual Difference', *Oxford Literary Review*, 8, 1–2, pp. 225–40

—— (1987) *In Other Worlds: Essays in Cultural Politics*, New York and London: Methuen

—— (1988) 'Can the Subaltern Speak?', in C. Nelson and L. Grossberg (eds), *Marxism and the Interpretation of Culture*, London: Macmillan, pp. 271–313

—— (1989a) 'A Response to "The Difference Within: Feminism and Critical Theory"', in E. Meese and A. Parker (eds), *The Difference Within: Feminism and Critical Theory*, Amsterdam/Philadelphia: John Benjamins Publishing Co., pp. 207–20

—— (1989b) 'The Political Economy of Women as Seen by a Literary Critic', in E. Weed (ed.), *Coming to Terms: Feminism, Theory, Politics*, New York: Routledge, pp. 218–29

—— (1990) *The Post-Colonial Critic: Interviews, Strategies, Dialogues*, ed. S. Harasym, London: Routledge

—— (1993) *Outside in the Teaching Machine*, New York: Routledge

Stender, N. (1977) *San Francisco Review of Books*, March, p. 19

Stephensen, P. R. (1969) 'The Foundations of Culture in Australia', in J. Barnes (ed.), *The Writer in Australia*, Melbourne: Oxford University Press, pp. 204–44

Stewart, S. (1984) *On Longing: Narratives of the Miniature, the Gigantic, the Souvenir, the Collection*, Baltimore: Johns Hopkins University Press

Thorne, T. (1976) 'The Image in the Mirror', *Australian*, 20 April

Todd, J. (1986) 'The Veiled Women in Freud's "Das Unheimliche"', *Signs*, 11, 3, Spring, pp. 519–28

Todorov, T. (1984) *Mikhail Bakhtin: the Dialogical Principle*, Minneapolis: University of Minnesota Press

Trinh, T. Minh-ha (1989) *Woman, Native, Other: Writing Postcoloniality and Feminism*, Bloomington: Indiana University Press

—— (1992) *Framer Framed*, London: Routledge

Ulmer, G. L. (1983) 'The Object of Post Criticism', in H. Foster (ed.), *Postmodern Culture*, London: Pluto Press, pp. 83–110

Vaughan, B. (1979) 'Verse Drenched in Tradition', *Australian Book Review*, February–March, p. 24

Virilio, P. and S. Lotringer (1983) *Pure War*, New York: Semiotext(e)

Viswanathan, G. (1989) *Masks of Conquest: Literary Study and British Rule in India*, New York: Columbia University Press

Wall, C. A. (ed.) (1989) *Changing Our Words: Essays on Criticism, Theory and Writing by Black Women*, New Brunswick: Rutgers University Press

Walwicz, A. (1982a) *Writing*, Melbourne: Rigmarole

—— (1982b) 'so small', in Narrative Course Team (eds), *Place to Place*, Geelong, Vic.: Deakin University Press, p. 84

—— (1983) 'Journeywomen', *Mattoid* 13, pp. 16–24

—— (1987a) Interview with U. Fitzgerald in *Mattoid*, 28, pp. 2–23

—— (1987b) *Europa*, Geelong, Vic.: Deakin University Media Unit

—— and Philip Hammial (1989a) *Travel/Writing*, Sydney: Angus & Robertson

—— (1989b) *Boat*, Sydney: Angus & Robertson

—— (1992a) *red roses*, Brisbane: University of Queensland Press

—— (1992b) 'The Politics of Experience. Ania Walwicz Interviewed by Jenny Digby', *Meanjin*, 51, 4, Summer, pp. 819–38

Widdowson, P. (ed.) (1982) *Re-Reading English*, London: Methuen

Wilden, A. (1968) *The Language of the Self*, Baltimore: Johns Hopkins University Press

Willis, S. (1990) *Specifying: Black Women Writing the American Experience*, London: Routledge

Wright, E. (1984) *Psychoanalytic Criticism*, London: Methuen

Yeatman, A. (1994) *Postmodernist Revisionings of the Political*, London: Routledge

Young, I. (1990) 'The Ideal of Community and the Politics of Difference', in L. J. Nicholson (ed.), *Feminism/Postmodernism*, New York: Routledge, pp. 300–23

Young, R. (1990) *White Mythologies: Writing History and the West*, London: Routledge

Zwicky, F. (1986) *The Lyre in the Pawnshop*, Nedlands: University of Western Australia

Index

Aborigines (Australian), 2, 30, 73; *see also* indigenous peoples
'Acrobat, The', 81; *see also* Kefala, A.
Acropolis Now, 8
Adorno, T. W., 20
'Alien, The', 81, 119; *see also* Kefala, A.
Alien Son, xii
'All Male Sauna, The', 89; *see also* Walwicz, A.
alterity, 32–6 *passim,* 39
Althusser, L., 60, 81
Anderson, B., 1, 18, 37, 47
Anderson, P., 38
Anglo-Celtic, 2, 3, 7–9 *passim,* 46, 116
Anthias, F., 2, 22, 47, 51–2
Antigone, 78; see also Sophocles
Ariès, P., 84
'Arts for a Multicultural Australia' policy, 16
Ashcroft, B., 34
'At the Pictures', 82; *see also* Kefala, A.
'Australia', 117; *see also* Walwicz, A.
Australia Council, 16–17
Australian Bicentennial Multicultural Foundation, 11
Australian culture, 9, 14, 65
Australian literature, 9, 10, 12, 14, 28, 73, 123, 130

Australian National Library, 11
Australian publishing, 15
authenticity, 10, 53–66 *passim*

Bakhtin, M., 24, 98–105, 117
Barthes, R., 71–2, 77, 112, 125
Beckett, S., 99
Belsey, C., 30, 54, 57
Bennett, T., 15
Benterrak, K., 73
Beyond the Echo, 6, 9; *see also* Gunew, S.; Mahyuddin, J.
Bhabha, H., 12, 32, 34–6, 39, 40, 43, 45
Bibliography of Australian Literature Project (BALP), 11
Bibliography of Australian Multicultural Writers, A, xiii, 10; *see also* Gunew, S.; Mahyuddin, J.
biculturalism, 2
Black studies, 41–3
Blonski, A., 7, 15–16
Boelhower, W., 1
'Boundary', 129–30; *see also Harbour Breathes, The*; Couani, A.
Brennan, T., 40–1
Brooks, P., 116
Burniston, S., 60
Byron, G., 78

Cappiello, R., xii, 24, 64–5, 93–110, 116
Carby, H., 43

Carter, P., 77
Castan, C., 111
Castles, S., 8
Chambers, R., 116
Chow, R., 33
Cixous, H., 55
Clifford, J., 33, 46
Clyne, M., 18
community, 17, 20–1
'Concert', 82; see also Kefala, A.
Couani, A., xi, 6, 9, 10, 24, 64, 111–31
Creed, B., 62, 109
Critique of Judgement, 27
cultural difference, 10, 13, 23, 39–40
Cultural Heritage Advisory Committee, 16–17
culture, *see* Australian culture; national cultures
Culture, Difference and the Arts, 18; *see also* Gunew, S.; Rizvi, F.
Cunningham, S., 15

'dad', 91; *see also* Walwicz, A.
Dante, 96
Davis, J., 73
Davis, N. Z., 102
Davison, D., 92
de Beauvoir, S., 55
de Lauretis, T., 44, 55–6, 66
de Man, P., 91
Deakin University, 6, 10–11
Deleuze, G., 12, 42, 58–9
Dell'oso, A.-M., 9
Delphy, C., 55
Department of Immigration, 60
Derrida, J., 11, 20, 27–9, 36, 39, 45, 53, 59, 63, 90–1, 115
'Des Tours de Babel', 90; *see also* Derrida, J.
Descartes, R., 29
'Detective, The', 121; *see also* Couani, A.
deterritorialisation, 12; *see also* Deleuze, G.; Guattari, F.
diaspora, 11, 19–21 *passim*
Dickens, B., 98
displaced persons, 3
Displacements, 7; *see also* Gunew, S.
Displacements 2, 7; *see also* Gunew, S.

Dostoievsky, F., 101
Doyle, B., 19
Durrell, L., 78
Dutton, G., 74
Dyer, R., 30–1

Eagleton, T., 14, 29, 37–8
Eco, U., 95
Eisenman, P., 125
Eliot, T. S., 123, 127
Ellmann, M., 75
Empire Writes Back, The, 34
English language, 18–19, 28, 72
English studies, 14, 19, 37–8
'Epilogue', 83; *see also* Kefala, A.
ethnic minority languages, 18–22 *passim*
ethnic minority writing, xii, 3, 11, 12, 23–4, 59–67, 71, 92, 111–12, 117; *see also* migrant writing; minor literature; minority literature; multicultural literature
ethnicity, 5, 11, 14–15, 22, 43, 45–52 *passim*
Eumenides, 81
Europa, 90; *see also* Walwicz, A.
'europe', 88; *see also* Walwicz, A.

Fanon, F., 12, 35
'Farewell Party', 81; *see also* Kefala, A.
feminism, 14, 21, 29, 42–4, 48, 53–9
Feminism and the Politics of Difference, 42; *see also* Gunew, S.; Yeatman, A.
Ferrier, C., 74
Fischer, M., 49
'Fold, The', 128–9; *see also* Couani, A.
Foucault, M., 32
framing, 27–8
Freadman, A., 54–5
Freud, S., 24, 62, 72, 86, 89, 116–18, 127
Function of Criticism, The, 37; *see also* Eagleton, T.

Gallop, J., 59, 111
Gatens, M., 48

Gates, Jr, H. L., 31
Geertz, C., 51
Genet, J., 98
Gibbs, A., 84
Giles, Z., 9
Gillett, S., 92
Girl/boy Talk, 89; *see also* Walwicz, A.
Griffith University, 16
Griffiths, G., 34
Grosz, E., 29–30, 44, 48, 56
Guattari, F., 12, 42, 58–9
Guillaume, M., 125
Gunew, S., xiii, 4, 6–7, 9–10, 11, 14–
    16, 18, 21, 42, 72, 83–4, 88, 113,
    119

Hall, S., 43–5
Haraway, D., 44–5, 48
Harbour Breathes, The, 125–9; *see
    also* Couani, A.
Harlow, B., 41
Hartman, G., 91
Hartsock, N., 33
Hatzimanolis, E., 84
Heidegger, M., 27
heimlich, 116–17; *see also* uncanny;
    unheimlich
Henriques, J., 30, 63
Hirst, P., 60
Hobsbawm, E., 37
Hodge, B., 73
Hoffmann, E. T. A., 118
Houbein, L., xiii; *see also Bibliogra-
    phy of Australian Multicultural
    Writers, A*
'Hour, The', 83; *see also* Kefala, A.
Hunter, I., 15
Hutcheon, L., 15, 50
hysteria, 89, 105–6, 114

'I', 89; see also Walwicz, A.
Imagined Communities, 18; *see also*
    Anderson, B.
immigration, 5, 7, 72
indigenous peoples, 2, 13; *see also*
    Aborigines
Inferno, 96
Institute for Cultural Policy Studies,
    16

Italy, 122, 125; *see also* Couani, A.

Jacobson, L., 92
Jacobus, M., 114
Jakubowitz, A., 6
JanMohammed, A., 33
Jardine, A., 30, 53–4, 59, 64–5
Jolley, E., 10
Joyce, J., 105
Julien, I., 31
Jung, C., 77
Junius, 75
Jupp, J., 3, 6
Jurgensen, M., 9

Kafka, F., 12, 42
Kamuf, P., 75–6
Kant, I., 27
Kaplan, C., 41–2
Karakostas-Seda, A., xiii; *see also Bib-
    liography of Australian Multi-
    cultural Writers, A*
Kee, P.-K., 48–9
Kefala, A., 24, 53, 64–5, 71–92, 119
Kim, D., 75, 76
Komninos, 9
Kramer, L., 130
Kristeva, J., 21, 24, 58, 61–3, 91, 101–
    5, 109, 113–15, 119

Lacan, J., 13, 60, 72, 77, 81, 87–8, 90,
    101, 104, 113–14, 117, 121, 128
Lautréamont, Comte de, 105
Lawson, H., 10
Lewitt, M., 81
Lindsay, E., 75–6
literature, *see* Australian literature;
    minor literature; minority litera-
    ture; multicultural literature
Lloyd, D., 33, 42, 64
Lloyd, G., 30
local knowledge, 44–6
Longley, K. O., xiii, 4, 14
Loriggio, F., 3–5
Lotringer, S., 66
Loukakis, A., 9
Lyotard, J.-F., 13, 29–30, 36, 57, 59,
    64–5, 125

MacCannell, J., 113, 121–2
Macklin, R., 95, 98–9
Mahyuddin, J., xiii, 6; *see also Beyond the Echo*
Mallarmé, S., 105
Malouf, D., 10, 73
Mani, L., 39
Markale, J., 108
Mathers, P., 98
'Memory', 78–83; *see also* Kefala, A.
Mercer, K., 31
Meredyth, D., 15
migrant, 5, 7, 10, 90, 92, 98, 116
migrant writing, xi–xii, 3–6, 9, 12, 23, 116–17; *see also* ethnic minority writing; minor literature; minority literature; multicultural literature
Milner, A., 38
minor literature, 12; *see also* Deleuze, G.; ethnic minority writing; Guattari, F., multicultural literature
minority literature, 12, 58–9; *see also* Deleuze, G., ethnic minority writing; Guattari, F.; multicultural literature
Mitchell, J., 89, 106
Modjeska, D., 73
Mohanty, C., 43
Moi, T., 55–6
Monash University, 11
mother tongue, 7, 91
Muecke, S., 73
Multicultural Advisory Committee for the Victorian Ministry for the Arts, 16
multicultural literature, xi–xii, 3, 9, 11, 14, 20–4, 116
multiculturalism, 6, 17, 22, 46–52 *passim*, 61

Nairn, T., 8
National Agenda for a Multicultural Australia, 5, 16
National Centre for Australian Studies, 11
national cultures, 14, 18–19, 30, 36–8, 47

NESB (non-English-speaking background), 7, 10, 16
'Never-Dead, The', 125; *see also* Couani, A.
'New World,' 88–9; *see also* Walwicz, A.
Nietzsche, F., 115
No Strangers Here, 60–1
non-Anglo-Celtic, 2, 8–9, 12, 17, 23, 30, 46, 116
non-English-speaking background, *see* NESB
Norris, C., 29, 53
nostalgia, 111–18 *passim*, 121–3, 127, 130

Oakley, B., 92
Oedipus, 78–9
Of Grammatology, 36; *see also* Derrida, J.
Off the Record, 85; *see also* Π. O.
Office of Multicultural Affairs (OMA), 5; *see also National Agenda for a Multicultural Australia*, 5
Oh Lucky Country, 93–110, 116; *see also* Cappiello, R.
Olivier, C., 79
'On the Job', 121; *see also* Couani, A.
oral history, 12, 23
Oresteia, 80
Orientalism, 30, 34; *see also* Said, E.
Outlaw, L., 48, 50
Outrider, 9
Owen, C., 89
Oxford History of Australia Literature, The, 130

Padolsky, E., xiii, 12
Pakeha, 2
Papaellinas, G., 9
Papastergiadis, N., 15, 77, 84
'Parergon, The', 27–8; *see also* Derrida, J.
'Parramatta Sestina', 127–8; *see also Harbour Breathes, The*; Couani, A.
Parry, B., 41
Pasolini, P., 98
Pearson, D., 48
'Photos', 89–90; *see also* Walwicz, A.

'Pillar of Rooms, The', 129–30; *see also Harbour Breathes, The*; Couani, A.
Π. O. (Pi. O.), 9, 85
Pivato, J., 11–12
'Poland', 87–8; *see also* Walwicz, A.
policy work, 5–6, 16–17, 22
Porter, D., 41
positionality, 5, 43–5, 116
post-colonialism, 12–13, 36, 38–42

Rabelais, F., 98
race, 46–52 *passim*
Rando, G., 93, 96, 99
red roses, 92; *see also* Walwicz, A.
Rich, A., 44
Richmond, M., 15
Ritsos, Y., 75
Rizvi, F., 6, 18, 51
Rizzo, S., 105
Roe, P., 73
Rothfield, P., 29
Rushdie, S., 40–1

Said, E., 12, 30–4, 36–8, 40–2, 46, 76
Sangari, K.-K., 41
Schaffer, K., 73
Schiavoni, F., 96, 99, 102–3
Schor, N., 56
'Science-Fiction City', 127; *see also Harbour Breathes, The*; Couani, A.
Scott, J., 56
second-generation writers, 8
Seferis, G., 75
Shapcott, T., 74
Silverman, K., 72, 85–90
Sivaramakrishnan, A., 33
Smith, B., 15
'so little', 85–7; *see also* Walwicz, A.
Sollors, W., 49–50, 73, 90, 105, 112–13
Sophocles, 79; *see also Antigone*
Spectator, 38
Spivak, G., 12, 31–3, 36, 39–40, 42–3, 90, 117
Stein, G., 84
Stender, N., 75
Stephensen, P., 131
Stewart, S., 111–12, 115, 122, 124

Stokes, G., 15
Striking Chords, xiii, 4, 14; *see also* Gunew, S.
subjectivity, 13, 30, 35, 39, 44, 54–67, 72–4, 81, 112–14
supplement, 12; *see also* Derrida, J.
Swift, J., 99
symbolic order, 13, 72–3, 90, 113–15, 127

Tatler, 38
Telling Ways, 6, 9, 10; *see also* Couani, A.; Gunew, S.
Thirsty Weather, 83; *see also* Kefala, A.
'Thirsty Weather', 83; *see also* Kefala, A.
Thorne, T., 74, 76
Tiffin, H., 34
Todorov, T., 100–2
Train, The, 120–2; *see also* Couani, A.
'translate', 90–2; *see also* Walwicz, A.
Trinh, T. M.-H., 33, 39, 41–5
Tristan and Isolde, 123

Ulmer, G., 117
uncanny, 62, 66, 112, 114–21 *passim*, 125–7, 130–1
unheimlich, 116, 118; *see also heimlich*; uncanny
universalism, 28–32, 42, 44–5

Vaughan, B., 75
'View, The', 120; *see also* Couani, A.
Virilio, P., 66
Viswanathan, G., 19

Wagner, R., 123
Walwicz, A., xii, 24, 64, 73, 76, 82, 84–92, 116–17
Wasteland, The, 123, 127
Waten, J., xii
Weedon, C., 60
Weltliteratur, 9
Were All Women Sex-mad?, 122–4; *see also* Couani, A.
Wilden, A., 72
'wogs', 87–8; *see also* Walwicz, A.
Wogs Out of Work, 8

'Women in Black, The', 82–3; *see also* Kefala, A.
women's writing, 9–10, 54–67 *passim*, 75
Wright, E., 89

'Xmas in the Bush', 120; *see also* Couani, A.

Yeatman, A., 21, 42
'Yesterday and Today', 120; *see also* Couani, A.
Young, I., 20–2
Young, R., 31, 34, 41
Yuval-Davis, N., 2, 22, 47, 51–2

Zwicky, F., 113